If One Uses It Lawfully

If One Uses It Lawfully

The Law of Moses and the Christian Life

Matthew E. Ferris

WIPF & STOCK · Eugene, Oregon

Wipf & Stock
An Imprint of Wipf and Stock Publishers
199 W. 8th Ave., Suite 3
Eugene, OR 97401

www.wipfandstock.com

PAPERBACK ISBN: 978-1-5326-4897-7
HARDCOVER ISBN: 978-1-5326-4898-4
EBOOK ISBN: 978-1-5326-4899-1

Manufactured in the U.S.A.

Unless otherwise indicated, all Scripture quotations are from The Holy Bible, English Standard Version® (ESV®), copyright © 2001 by Crossway Bibles, a publishing ministry of Good News Publishers. Used by permission.

Contents

Abbreviations

AB	Anchor Bible
ASV	American Standard Version
ICC	International Critical Commentary
JETS	Journal of the Evangelical Theological Society
LW	Luther's Works
NASB	New American Standard Bible
NCBC	New Century Bible Commentary
NICNT	New International Commentary on the New Testament
NIGTC	New International Greek Testament Commentary
NKJV	New King James Version
NSBT	New Studies in Biblical Theology
SGBC	Story of God Bible Commentary
SiBL	Studies in Biblical Literature
WBC	Word Biblical Commentary

1

Why Then the Law?

God, as husband of the gospel church, claims from his people inward affection and love, and accepts them only who worship him in spirit and in truth. In the Mosaic covenant it was otherwise; there he appeared chiefly as a temporal prince, and therefore gave laws intended rather to direct the outward conduct, than to regulate the actings of the heart.

—John Erskine[1]

WHEN WE SPEAK OF God's law, we encompass a large span of biblical territory. The question Paul asks of the Galatians, "Why then the law?",[2] still has great relevance for believers today. The topic continues to divide commentators and Christians across the theological spectrum. The scope of my survey will focus on the question of whether the Mosaic law has a continuing role in the life of the Christian. If it does, what is that role? The way the law became embedded in the fabric of Western culture illustrates the fraught relationship many still have with the law. In early America, "blue laws" came about as attempts to control what shouldn't be done

---

1. Erskine, "Sinai Covenant," 4–5.
2. Gal 3:19.

1

on Sundays. "Among other things, there was to be no traveling, cooking, making beds, sweeping homes, running, walking in the garden, or cutting hair on Sunday."[3]

Implicit in this is a change to consider Sunday as the new Sabbath. But this kind of thing comes with a picking and choosing of what applies today and what doesn't. Numbers 15 tells the story about a man who gathered sticks on the Sabbath day. Moses waited for God's direction concerning the man. The penalty for breaking the Sabbath was death, and so on God's order the community executed the man. I'm sure everyone who decides to use Sunday afternoon to catch up on yard work is very glad that is not enforced today!

Someone may protest that this is a Jewish law, no longer applicable today. This illustrates exactly the kind of decisions we make when we talk about the law. Blue laws were a tacit admission that not all the stipulations of the Mosaic law apply today. Even in early America, someone guilty of cooking or sweeping on Sunday may have incurred church discipline, but these were not capital crimes, as Sabbath-breaking was in Israel. Society has modified and accommodated these laws in numerous ways, but in so doing, it has strayed from God's intent in giving them.

One of the more common views on God's law today is that the Ten Commandments (also called the Decalogue) are still in force. This view holds that, even if the other parts of the Mosaic law aren't for us, the Ten Commandments are. Various theological perspectives share this view, even when they don't see eye to eye on other matters. I'll term this perspective the rule-of-life view, since the view holds that the Ten Commandments remain a standard, a rule of life by which Christians in this age should live. We should order our lives according to the Decalogue, and in so doing we please God. That's a crude synopsis of this view, and I'll unpack this much more in the following pages. There are other assumptions underlying this view, and the question is, are those assumptions valid?

---

3. Harline, *Sunday*, 286.

The rule-of-life view of the law does not account for the definitive statements Paul makes about it. He proclaims our death to the law, contrasts it with the Spirit, and teaches that spiritual fruitfulness doesn't depend on the law. Rather than upholding the law (as Paul claims his teaching does in Rom 3:31), the insistence on a continuing obligation to the law for Christians, in fact, weakens it. It separates commandment from curse, and puts the believer under obligation to the command, but discharges the curse. This represents an "unlawful" use of the law. I am aware that rule-of-life theologians are not monolithic in their approach to the question of law. Whatever variations there are, the dominant theme is that the obligation to the Decalogue continues in the age of grace.

The New Testament never presents the law as a rule or standard for the believer in this age. Rather, Christ himself is the standard, the goal, the guide, and the one Christians look to and dwell upon. A common objection is that if we are not under obligation to the Ten Commandments, we are antinomian, or literally "against the law." The word "antinomian" will be addressed more fully in later chapters, but it is too simplistic to suggest that declaring Christians as not under obligation to the Ten Commandments is to set oneself against God's law. Paul himself faced similar accusations: "And why not do evil that good may come?—as some people slanderously charge us with saying."[4] The apostle makes clear that our sinful flesh is capable and ready to turn the freedom from law into license. But he never presents the law as a safeguard against such a thing. On the contrary, he warns his converts specifically of the dangers of applying the law to their lives as Christians. The latter chapters of Galatians clearly set this forth.

The bugbear of antinomianism is a frequent obstacle in any discussion of the believer's position with respect to the law. For some, if one suggests freedom from the law for the believer, this means not only a license to sin as freely as we wish but also an encouragement to do so. Some, indeed, recognize that affirming the believer's position as out from under the law is not the same as indifference to the pursuit of holiness. The former position "has

4. Rom 3:8.

3

been called 'doctrinal antinomianism' as opposed to 'practical antinomianism.'"[5] Despite that distinction, the category of "antinomian" is a broad brush to caricature freedom from the law. Historians recognize that it's too facile to categorize various parties as pro-law, and thus good, versus anti-law, and thus bad. In an understatement that borders on sarcasm, the ESV Study Bible notes, "Exactly how the law applies to the New Testament believer is a matter of some debate."[6] It is certainly a matter of debate, but applying the label "antinomian" is too often a barrier to understanding someone's position, rather than contributing to greater clarity.

There are several reasons why some hold the view of a continuing obligation to the law in the Christian life, but they do not stand up under scrutiny. I show in the following pages that the position of Christian freedom from the law is the only scripturally consistent one. It is the only one that "upholds the law." Christians have an imperative to holiness, to be transformed into Christlikeness. But the means of doing so at this stage of salvation history is not the Ten Commandments.

Presenting the law as a rule of life or the standard of conduct is assigning a purpose to it that God did not intend for this age, and is using the law "unlawfully," as Paul warns against in 1 Timothy 1:8–11. It is not for the just, and Christians—because of their position in Christ—are just before God. To insist that Christians today are under obligation to the Ten Commandments redefines what the law is, and its purpose. An obligation to the law, but without any consequence for breaking it, introduces a category of law unknown in Scripture. The commands of the Decalogue then become a kind of vaccination with an inactivated strain of law. Denatured of the consequence that they had under the Mosaic economy, this reduces the law's commands to suggestions. But it can also obscure our understanding of the way Paul does use the law.

Some are apt to think that Christian living is best exemplified by striking a balance between law and license, of walking a kind of middle ground between them. But this, too, is a misunderstanding.

5. Bayes, *Weakness of the Law*, 4.
6. *English Standard Version*, 2326.

The apostle Paul warns and fulminates against legalism as much as he does against license. We err if we imagine that growth in Christian maturity is a matter of having just enough law to keep us from falling into sin. We cannot measure sanctification on the same axis with law. To arrive at a coherent position means we need to look beyond a list of prohibitions and commands situated in the old covenant. The scriptural record yields a few principles:

1) Morality is not equal to law keeping. Before God gave the law, there were definite moral requirements, as there are after it. Indeed, when compared to the exhortations and commands of the New Testament, the law of Moses represents a lowest common denominator, but not a distinctively Christian approach to holiness.

2) The headship of Christ puts the believer in a completely different realm from that of Adam. This realm is one where the law is not a factor, not a reference point for pleasing God. This is not because Christians are free from morality (quite the contrary), but because, as raised up and seated with Christ in the heavenly places, this new identity means we do not pursue conformity to him by reference to the law's commands. David Peterson summarizes this: "Sanctification in the New Testament is an integral part of the redemptive work of Jesus Christ. It is regularly portrayed as a once-for-all, definitive act and primarily has to do with the holy status and position of those who are 'in Christ.'"[7]

3) The Scriptures present an unfolding of God's plan, often called the history of salvation. Progressive revelation is another aspect of this history. We know things that previous ages did not know because they were not revealed, or we know them more fully than they did. These developments in salvation history have definite consequences for believers. The law and our relationship to it is one of those consequences.

4) The New Testament enjoins holiness and growth into Christlikeness for believers in this age, but the means of accomplishing that growth does not come through the law of Moses. Having redeemed us, God does not lead us back to the law for

---

7. Peterson, *Possessed By God*, 24.

a Spirit-enabled keeping of the Ten Commandments. He aims to take us beyond this, to conform us not to statutes, but to the Savior.

A major thesis of this book is this: *The Ten Commandments are by no means inconsistent with the will of God for his redeemed people, but they are not coextensive with it. The New Testament points the believer to Jesus as the embodiment and pattern of God's wisdom.* To see the Decalogue as the summation of God's will for mankind leads to the conclusion that there is no higher standard, nothing beyond that a believer should aspire to. Two immediate objections to this are that it does not present the person of Christ in proper biblical relief, and it minimizes (if not ignores) the developments in salvation history that are clear as one moves from old covenant to new. In the following chapters, I explicate this thesis by interacting with Scripture and various commentators upon it.

Whether we can articulate it well or not, we all have a position on the law and how it relates to us as believers in Christ. Some strive to live by the Ten Commandments, filtered perhaps through the Sermon on the Mount. Others know that they relate to God on the basis of grace, but they wouldn't be comfortable saying that they are entirely free from the law's commands. As a result, many live in a theological no-man's-land. They know they are, in some sense, free from the condemnation of law because of Jesus, but they don't exactly know what to make of the various (and seemingly contradictory) references to the law in the New Testament.

A perennial danger for believers is that we love law. Not in the way the psalmist wrote, "Oh how I love your law!", but in the sense of the Pharisee in Luke 18, who stood praying and said, "God, I thank you that I am not like other men." He then goes on to detail his law-abiding life, the things he doesn't do, and the things he does. He imagined he had done what God requires of him. If we're honest with ourselves, we'll admit that we like the clear expectations of completing a list, checking a box. And when we've checked all the boxes, it's very tempting to think that God has become our debtor. He must bless me because I've done all these things! That tendency is deep within our sinful hearts, and it's very easy to fall into such a mindset. But God owes us nothing, certainly not for our obedience or adherence to statutes, no matter how good those statutes are. This is one of the dangers of measuring our Christian lives by law, even the Decalogue.

The apostle Paul (who, more than any other biblical writer, speaks of the law) has not made the task an easy one. His pronouncements about the law are both extensive and varied. At times he speaks in negative ways, other times he speaks positively about the law. Arriving at coherence can be difficult indeed. The plethora of books on the proper understanding of Paul and the number of scholars who have made the apostle to the gentiles their area of expertise are evidence that his theology is a formidable topic. More than any other New Testament writer, readers of Scripture must wrestle with Paul if they are to arrive at any understanding of law.

Justification by faith, entirely apart from the law, is settled doctrine and uncontroversial. All points on the Protestant theological spectrum agree on these facts of justification. One does not get into God's family by reference to the law, nor by doing what it commands. Paul delineates these truths in the first several chapters of Romans with clarity and force. The question is, once in the family, what is the continuing use of the law? The rule-of-life view's answer is that, although the law plays no part in our justification, it is the instrument God uses to sanctify us.

As important as it is to see the ground of our justification as entirely apart from the law, some have also drawn a distinction between justification and sanctification that is too sharp. Confusion on the role of law in Christian life is, in one sense, a result of considering sanctification in a wholly different category from justification. We must see sanctification as flowing from justification organically. This is how the New Testament treats it. Peterson, again, stresses the importance of seeing sanctification as "definitive"; that is, that it accompanies salvation: "Several texts point to the fact that God sanctifies his people once and for all, through the work of Christ on the cross. Other texts link sanctification with conversion or baptism into Christ, highlighting the work of the Holy Spirit through the gospel, consecrating believers to God as

his holy people under the new covenant."[8] Sanctification is both
a possession and a goal. We pursue the goal because we already
belong to Christ, and we do so by continually going back to the position of our identity in Christ, as justified and seated with Christ
in the heavenly places. A view of sanctification as separate from
justification, something we pursue on an entirely different basis
from how we are justified before God, is an implicit "yes" to the
apostles' question: "having begun by the Spirit, are you now being
perfected by the flesh?"[9]

Previous eras of Christian thought are valuable to us and
help sharpen our understanding of the Scriptures. But one should
be careful about ceding biblical ground to a system, even if it has
commendable aspects. I greatly esteem the Reformation heritage,
but it should not be the case that we yield allegiance to a view only
because of what it goes with, or who expounds it. If the position is
biblically defensible, that is certainly a reason to hold it; if it is not,
then the fact that it is a tenet of a larger hermeneutical framework
should not constrain belief. This is the essence of what the rule-of-
life position has done with respect to the law and Christian obligation to it. Whether it is a confessional statement or suppositions
about the character and nature of God, these assumptions have at
times been the overruling factors in rule-of-life adherents' position on the law, rather than allowing Scripture to speak.

Paul doubtless engages in wordplay when he speaks of using the law "lawfully." His accusation of an "unlawful" use of law
goes beyond justification. It is clear that the apostle is concerned
to warn Timothy about applying law to those already justified. The
law had no part in procuring life in Christ; neither is it the means
of making us more like Christ. The following chapters look at the
Mosaic law from various angles. Only by examining its original
purpose, the recipients of the law, and (importantly) to consider
the apostolic treatment of it, can we arrive at how the Christian
should regard the law. The task of any reader of Scripture must
be to look at the whole of God's revelation and to determine what

8. Peterson, *Possessed By God*, 13.
9. Gal 3:3.

God requires of us now, in this age. The sum of this examination is that the believer's pattern for Christian life is not a what, but who.

2

Law: Its Definition and Extent

When the Law is being used correctly, it does nothing but reveal sin, work wrath, accuse, terrify, and reduce the minds of men to the point of despair. And that is as far as the Law goes.

—Luther[1]

How "Law" is used in Scripture

THE READER OF SCRIPTURE will soon see that the word "law" can take several different meanings in its pages. When we speak of the Christian's relationship to the law it is important to understand which meaning is in view. The Jewish nation, the first recipients of the law, principally understood the law to be the first five books of the Hebrew Bible, the Pentateuch. It is in this sense that Jesus refers to "the Law and the prophets" in the Sermon on the Mount.[2] Often, the name of Moses is a synonym for the law: "They said to him, 'Why then did Moses command one to give a certificate of divorce and to send her away?' He said to them, 'Because of your hardness of heart Moses allowed you to divorce your wives, but

1. *LW* 26:313.
2. Matt 7:12.

from the beginning, it was not so.'"[3] The command referred to as coming from Moses is Deuteronomy 24:1, a part of the Pentateuch.

Moses was the agent through whom God delivered the law to Israel, but the Jews did not assume Moses to be the author of that law. When Jesus meets the two disciples on the Emmaus road after his resurrection, he instructs them, "Beginning with Moses and all the prophets."[4] What the Jewish people refer to as "Torah" are these first five books of the Bible. Within Judaism, it is difficult to overestimate their foundational nature. The prophets who ministered later in Israel were in large part doing nothing but calling the people back to obedience to these five books.

The law as specifically applicable to the people of Israel is also a fact that is clear from the Old Testament.

> For you are a people holy to the LORD your God. The LORD your God has chosen you to be a people for his treasured possession, out of all the peoples who are on the face of the earth . . . You shall therefore be careful to do the commandment and the statutes and the rules that I command you today.[5]

This consciousness as a people set apart, recipients of God's law, is at the heart of Jewish identity. The psalmist writes, "He declares his word to Jacob, his statutes and rules to Israel. He has not dealt thus with any other nation; they do not know his rules."[6] Because Israel is God's chosen people, the nation he redeemed from bondage in Egypt, this is one reason they received God's law.

To be a Jew was to be in a covenant relationship with God, and the law is the substance, the treaty of that covenant. Harry Gersh writes, "The traditional relationship of God to Israel the People, and of God to each individual Jew, was that of Law-Giver to Law-follower. The prescriptions, set down mainly in Deuteronomy, Leviticus, and Exodus, are the basis for the civil, religious, and moral

---

3. Matt 19:7–8.
4. Luke 24:47.
5. Deut 7:6, 11.
6. Ps 147:19–20.

laws that governed the total life of the Jews and differentiated them from the Gentiles."[7] The law was given to a specific people in a specific land. Several statements in Deuteronomy make this clear:

> "I will tell you the whole commandment and the statutes and the rules that you shall teach them, that they may do them in the land that I am giving them to possess."[8]

> "Now this is the commandment—the statutes and the rules—that the LORD your God commanded me to teach you, that you may do them in the land to which you are going over, to possess it."[9]

> "For you are to cross over the Jordan, to go in to take possession of the land that the LORD your God is giving you. And when you possess it and live in it, you shall be careful to do all the statutes and the rules that I am setting before you today."[10]

> "For it is no empty word for you, but your very life, and by this word you shall live long in the land that you are going over the Jordan to possess."[11]

Indeed, much of the law that God gave to the nation was for the time when they would be in the land, no longer wandering in the wilderness. David Dorsey offers the following: "The corpus [of the law] was designed to regulate the lives of a people living in the distinctive geographical and climatic conditions found in the southern Levant, and many of the regulations are inapplicable, unintelligible, or even nonsensical outside that regime. Take, for example, the law in Exod 29:22 regulating the offering of the 'fat-tail' of the ram. This ruling would be unfulfillable for people dwelling in the many regions of the world where the Palestinian fat-tailed sheep, with its unique ten- to fifteen-pound fatty tail

7. Gersh, *Sacred Books of the Jews*, 56.
8. Deut 5:31.
9. Deut 6:1.
10. Deut 11:31–32.
11. Deut 32:47.

is unknown—to say nothing of the tribes of the earth who have never seen a sheep of any sort."[12]

If the application of the law to Israel in the land is undeniable, it is likewise true that, for Christianity, the Pentateuch is also foundational. The fundamental doctrines of God as creator, the Trinity, the proto-evangel of Genesis 3:15, substitutionary atonement, the covenant with Abraham—all these are in the first third of Genesis. The Christian faith rests upon the historical revelation found in the law—the Torah—and so every Christian acknowledges the position and abiding relevance of these books. It is interesting to note that, among those who cast doubt on the biblical record, two things often deemed to be myth in the Hebrew Bible are the idea of historical Adam and the Genesis flood. Yet the Lord Jesus affirms these two as historical facts. In accepting Jesus' view of these events, the Christian also accepts the validity of the Torah for today.

The apostle Paul affirms this as well when he writes, "For whatever was written in former days was written for our instruction, that through endurance and the encouragement of the Scriptures, we might have hope."[13] It is important to note this because it is all too common to find the sentiment that, if one rejects an obligation to the law for the believer of today, or claims that the law forms no rule of life for the Christian, this is tantamount to a rejection of the Old Testament witness. It is odd to find someone such as Walter C. Kaiser opine, "The value which a Christian assigns to the Old Testament will be directly dependent on the answer he gives to the law-grace question."[14] Kaiser apparently means to say that, if one holds to freedom from the law for the believer, it is inevitably accompanied with placing a low value on the Old Testament. Such a conclusion is not warranted. I have often heard the richest teaching on biblical typology from the Old Testament among those who held the believer to be free from the law's obligation. There is not disagreement over the importance of the Old

---

12. Dorsey, "Law of Moses," 325.

13. Rom 15:4.

14. Kaiser, "Leviticus 18:5 and Paul," 20.

Testament, but over the way in which we interact with the law as New Testament believers.

A common way of dealing with this difficulty is to divide the law into categories of applicability. These are usually classed as moral, civil, and ceremonial. Along with these categories, Bible students have also noted distinct uses of the law. We can diagram these as follows:

Civil		
Ceremonial		
Moral		
To regulate life in Israel	To convict of sin and point to Christ	As a rule of life for Christians
First Use	Second Use	Third Use

I will further explore both the categories and the uses for their validity. If one accepts these categories of law, it will lead to the rule-of-life view.

In addition to law as Pentateuch, another meaning of law found in scripture is the Ten Commandments, or the Decalogue. When Paul uses the term law, he is at times referring not to the five books of Moses, or even to the whole of their commands, but only to the Ten Commandments. Paul affirms, "For I would not have known what it is to covet if the law had not said, 'You shall not covet.'"[15] Clearly, the apostle is not talking about the entire Pentateuch, but only the last of the Ten Commandments, which he refers to as "the law."

The Ten Commandments as law becomes important in any discussion of their continuing role in the Christian life, because in the "law as rule of life" perspective, the "moral law" is equated with the Ten Commandments. But there are certainly moral aspects of the law that live outside the Decalogue. It is this narrower

15. Rom 7:7.

sense, of the Decalogue being the equivalent of the moral law, that is of prime importance in any discussion of the place of law in the Christian life. The rule-of-life view holds that God has abrogated the dietary or civil laws, and it is only the Decalogue that remains in force as an aid to sanctification. This involves assumptions and redefinitions of law that I will explore further.

We also note a somewhat parenthetical use of "law," as a synonym for "principle." Thus Paul says, "I find it to be a law that when I want to do right, evil lies close at hand."[16] Substitute the word "principle" here, and it becomes clear what the apostle is saying. Think of the "law of gravity" and this is an analogy. Leon Morris affirms that, aside from the clear references to the Mosaic law, Paul sometimes uses the word in this more general sense: "In addition to these more or less straightforward uses of the term Paul has a number of other expressions. He can speak of 'the law of faith' and of 'the law of works' ([Romans] 3:27; NIV translates with 'principle,' and Hodge thinks the word here means 'a rule of action')."[17] Not all agree on the extent of this. Some, indeed, see references to the Mosaic law, where others assign this more general sense to the word.

The Unity of the Law

While it seems logical (and is common) to divide the law into the categories of moral, civil, and ceremonial, these divisions are artificial. At best, certain texts imply these categories, but they are nowhere stipulated in Scripture. Schreiner identifies the challenge of deconstructing these three categories: "Indeed, it is quite difficult to distinguish what is 'moral' and 'ceremonial' in the law. For instance, the law forbidding the taking of interest is clearly a moral mandate (Exod. 22:25), but this law was addressed to Israel as an agricultural society."[18] If this is part of the moral law, then

---

16. Rom 7:21.

17. Morris, *Romans*, 144.

18. Schreiner, *40 Questions*, 90.

Christians cannot put their money in interest-bearing accounts, if they believe the moral law continues in force even as the civil and ceremonial laws are no longer authoritative. The prohibition on interest is also not included in the Ten Commandments. Is it moral? Yes, but is it then binding on believers today? I am not aware of anyone who believes so.

Peter Gentry and Stephen Wellum argue this inherent unity is in the Old Testament text, quite apart from any New Testament commentary on the law.

> It is common to categorize and classify the laws as (a) moral, (b) civil, and (c) ceremonial, but this classification is foreign to the material and imposed upon it from the outside rather than arising from the material and being clearly marked by the literary structure of the text. In fact, the ceremonial, civil, and moral laws are all mixed together, not only in the Judgments or ordinances but in the Ten Words as well (the Sabbath may be properly classified as ceremonial). Those who claim the distinction between ceremonial, civil, and moral law do so because they want to affirm that the ceremonial (and in some cases, civil) laws no longer apply but the moral laws are eternal. This is an inaccurate representation of Scripture at this point.[19]

Even those who argue for a continuing obligation to the law recognize this. Knox Chamblin, who advocates the rule-of-life view of the Decalogue, admits the threefold division to be problematic: "Such a distinction can be misleading, because both OT and NT normally use the term 'law' to speak of the whole Mosaic Law rather than a particular aspect of it; and moral, ceremonial, and civil laws are inextricably bound together in the OT, each kind being intelligible and operable only in relation to the other two."[20]

While we can see the separate application of various Old Testament laws (this one speaks to the regulation of commerce, that one to family relationships), do these separate applications

---

19. Gentry and Wellum, *Kingdom Through Covenant*, 355.
20. Chamblin, "Law of Moses," 183.

allow for the categorization of laws so as to set only some of them aside? We may say these are traditional categories, but they are without explicit directives in the Scripture. Jason Meyer agrees:

> The NT itself does not make these three distinctions, and no one living under the law of Moses seriously thought they could pick which parts were binding and which were optional. God's law comes as a set with no substitutions. Therefore, exegetes should not read the three distinctions into NT texts that speak of the law as a singular entity.[21]

Treating the law as a unit continues into the New Testament. Paul speaks only of law, not of moral, ceremonial, or civil. And indeed when he makes his most definitive statements about believers released from obligation to law, he draws his examples from those very portions styled "the moral law." In Romans 7, Paul quotes the tenth commandment, "You shall not covet," and goes on to say, "But sin, seizing an opportunity through the commandment, produced in me all kinds of covetousness." Rule-of-life commentators give this point too little weight in their discussions of law. The apostolic treatment of the law addresses it as a unit and does not allow for dispensing with one part while retaining others.

Reading Paul's letter to the Galatian churches, it's clear there were big problems he was addressing, and none bigger than their confusion about the function and use of the law. To dissuade them from any notion that some law was acceptable, he quotes from Deuteronomy 27:26, emphasizing the unity of the entire law: "Cursed be everyone who does not abide by all things written in the Book of the Law, and do them."[22] A bit later, confronting those who believe circumcision to be necessary, Paul warns, "I testify again to every man who accepts circumcision that he is obligated to keep the whole law."[23] Paul takes an all or nothing approach to the law with the Galatians. C. H. Hogg and W. E. Vine comment, "The law is not to be conceived as a bundle of separate strands,

21. Meyer, *End of the Law*, 282.
22. Gal 3:10.
23. Gal 5:3.

whereof if one be broken the rest may still remain intact, but rather as a sheet of glass which, if it be broken in any part, is broken as a whole."[24] Jesus affirms this unity also: "For truly, I say to you, until heaven and earth pass away, not an iota, not a dot, will pass from the Law until all is accomplished."[25] It's difficult to find anything but a unified treatment of the law in what Jesus says.

Why then the category of moral law? If the laws relating to morality are distinct from those governing Jewish society, this supports maintaining these laws as an ongoing standard. Morality is not done away with in the New Testament, and laws that appear to be moral in nature must surely continue. No one would oppose morality or holy living. The assumption behind this is that the Ten Commandments are the pinnacle of moral instruction, that God has provided no higher standard for mankind, or for believers. I defer the full discussion of this to chapter 3, but the apostolic evidence ("We are released from the law"[26]) doesn't support the view that morality must always rest on the law.

The concept of the moral law as a separate category is perhaps the largest factor behind all claims of Christian obligation to law. It is a first principle such that all other decisions about how to deal with the law must fit under this rubric. But the biblical foundation for this hypothesis is wanting. At best it comes through inference only. At worst, it denies the explicit statements concerning the beginning of the law, its duration, and the end of our obligation to it. For many who hold the rule-of-life view, their basis for this is in fact confessional, rather than scriptural. Confessions can provide helpful summaries of biblical teaching, but they are not Scripture, and should not be elevated to the same authority.

24. Hogg and Vine, *Galatians*, 240–41.

25. Matt 5:18.

26. Rom 7:6.

A Trans-Covenantal Argument for Law?

Rule-of-life proponents acknowledge that there isn't a strict three-fold division in the text of Scripture, but believe there is a way the inspired writers refer to the law that allows us to say that obligation to it remains. In other words, the apostolic references to the Ten Commandments allow one to speak of the "moral law." A major argument for the continuation of the moral law through the new-covenant era rests on this assumption. Although God gave the moral law formal revelation at Sinai in the Ten Commandments, it precedes that event and is thus trans-covenantal (I use the term moral law only for the sake of pursuing this argument). That is, since the Decalogue is God's moral imperative, it cannot be that he limits it only to the Mosaic covenant. The *Westminster Larger Catechism* sets this forth in question 92:

> Q: What did God first reveal to man as the rule of his obedience?
>
> A: The rule of obedience revealed to Adam in the state of his innocence, and to all mankind in him, besides a special command not to eat of the fruit of the tree of the knowledge of good and evil, was the moral law.[27]

It is clear that the Westminster divines did not view the prohibition on eating of the tree as itself the moral law, but separate from it. It is an inference that, when God placed Adam in the Garden, he gave him this moral law at that time, but Scripture is silent on such an event. Edward Fisher's *The Marrow of Modern Divinity* says much the same as Westminster: "Adam heard as much (of the law) in the garden, as did Israel at Sinai; only in fewer words, and without thunder."[28] "For the general substance of the duty, the law delivered on Mount Sinai, and formerly engraven on man's heart, was one and the same; so that at Mount Sinai the Lord delivered

---

27. Westminster Assembly, *Larger Catechism*, Q. 92.
28. Fisher, *Modern Divinity*, 31.

no new thing, only it came more gently to Adam before his fall, but after his fall came thunder with it."[29]

Fisher is no outlier in what he affirms. Along with the Catechism, *The Westminster Confession of Faith* says, "God gave to Adam a law, as a covenant of works, by which he bound him and all his posterity to personal, entire, exact, and perpetual obedience, promised life upon the fulfilling, and threatened death upon the breach of it, and endued him with power and ability to keep it."[30] It is also clear that, after the fall (sometimes referred to as the postlapsarian era) and the promise of a redeemer in Genesis 3:15, the obligation to obey this law remained. The *Confession* again states, "This law, after his fall, continued to be a perfect rule of righteousness; and, as such, was delivered by God upon Mount Sinai, in ten commandments, and written in two tables."[31]

Wesley, in fact, goes beyond the claim of the Westminster theologians by suggesting that there was a giving of the law to the angelic hosts before creation: "But we may indeed trace its original higher still, even beyond the foundation of the world, to that period, unknown indeed to men, but doubtless enrolled in the annals of eternity, when 'the morning stars [first] sang together,' being newly called into existence."[32] Here, too, Wesley does not support his claim with biblical evidence. The quotation from the book of Job shows indeed that angels predated earth's creation, but it says nothing about the law.

There are difficulties in such a view. First, as noted previously, the division of law into categories of moral or immoral is impossible to maintain from Scripture. Attempts to lift the Ten Commandments out of their original covenantal context do not do justice to the text, and in fact downgrade their role in Israel's history. Gentry and Wellum again comment, "The Ten Words form the heart of the covenant between God and Israel at Sinai . . . the Book of the Covenant is what forges Israel into a nation. It is her national

---

29. Fisher, *Modern Divinity*, 57.
30. Westminster Assembly, *Confession of Faith*, 19.1.
31. Westminster Assembly, *Confession of Faith*, 19.2.
32. Wesley, "Use of the Law," 307.

constitution, so to speak."[33] Locating its provenance in the Garden of Eden assigns a new and different meaning to what occurred at Sinai. Adam and Eve, moreover, were not promised eternal life. As F. W. Grant says, "If I open Genesis, I find no hope of heaven held out to him there, no idea of being raised above the estate in which he was created. I find no works enjoined for which he was to be rewarded; one prohibition only of a thing which would have had no moral character attaching to it, had it not been forbidden. Created very good, he was to keep his first estate, not seek a new one."[34]

Some have argued, as Bruce Waltke does, that the Decalogue is the only portion of the law written by God himself, the only part deposited in the Ark of the Covenant, and thus "not restricted to geography or history, to time and space."[35] Waltke argues that this, therefore, gives it a unique position. However, it is one thing to categorize the Old Testament commands and to recognize a distinct position given to the Decalogue within the Mosaic covenant (as Gentry and Wellum point out, the centrality of the Decalogue within the covenant between God and Israel is beyond question), but it is another thing to claim that this position is an abiding and enduring one that both predates Moses and remains in force after the bringing in of the new covenant.

If the inscription of the Decalogue by God himself on tables of stone sets them to be an abiding rule for believers in the church, it is odd to find Paul saying, "what once had glory has come to have no glory at all, because of the glory that surpasses it. For if what was being brought to an end came with glory, much more will what is permanent have glory."[36] Thus, contra Waltke, Paul viewed the Ten Commandments not only as part of the Mosaic covenant, but the end of their obligation with the arrival of the new covenant. He expressly designates the tablets of stone as brought to an end, and the new covenant as having permanence.

---

33. Gentry and Wellum, *Kingdom through Covenant,* 327–28.

34. Grant, *Numerical Bible,* 220–21.

35. Waltke, "Kingdom of God," 83.

36. 2 Cor 3:10–11.

The trans-covenantal view of the law is part of the fabric of covenant (Reformed) theology. The *Westminster Confession* states, "Man, by his fall, having made himself uncapable of life by that covenant, the Lord was pleased to make a second, commonly called the covenant of grace."[37] It is clear, then, that by this viewpoint, the various covenants such as the Abrahamic, Mosaic, Davidic, or even the new covenant, are not to be thought of as distinct covenants, but instead as part of this single, overarching covenant: "There are not therefore two covenants of grace, differing in substance, but one and the same, under various dispensations."[38]

The implications of this are extensive. The *Confession* stresses continuity in God's dealings with man, but this comes at the expense of appreciating the profound discontinuity between what God set forth in prior ages and what we now enjoy in the new covenant. As David A. Weir comments, "Thus we see that the classical distinctions between the Old Testament and the New Testament (and the Mosaic Old Covenant and the Christian New Covenant) are subsumed under one covenant, the postlapsarian covenant of grace."[39] Weir further notes that Christ took the place of Adam as federal head, faithfully obeying the first covenant of works where the first Adam failed: "The postlapsarian covenant of grace is really therefore the prelapsarian covenant of works in disguise, but a new Adam (Christ) was needed to keep the covenant which God had established with man at the beginning of the world. Once the prelapsarian covenant of works is established, it can never be broken."[40]

Acknowledging the covenant concept as a helpful tool, Wellum nevertheless urges caution if this idea is pressed too far:

> If we are not careful, however, the notion of the "covenant of grace" may be misleading, because Scripture does not speak of only one covenant with different administrations. Rather, Scripture speaks in terms of a plurality of covenants (e.g., Gal 4:24; Eph 2:12; Heb 8:7–13), which

37. Westminster Assembly, *Confession of Faith*, 7.3.
38. Westminster Assembly, *Confession of Faith*, 7.6.
39. Weir, *Federal Theology*, 5.
40. Weir, *Federal Theology*, 5.

are all part of the progressive revelation of the one plan of God that is ultimately fulfilled in the new covenant. In reality, the "covenant of grace" is a comprehensive theological category, not a biblical one.[41]

Wellum is speaking of baptism in this context, but his point is equally valid for one's view of the law: "Emphasis on the continuity of the covenant of grace has led them [covenant theologians] to flatten the covenantal differences and thus to misconstrue the nature of the new covenant community."[42]

The progressive revelation of the one plan of God means that things of prior ages and covenants are very often replaced in the new covenant. We do not celebrate the Passover as a Christian ordinance because the reality it signified has arrived. For Christ, our Passover lamb, was sacrificed for us.[43] Paul understood the believer's obligation to the Mosaic law, including the Decalogue, to have come to an end, because the Mosaic covenant was brought to an end, supplanted by the new covenant.

When Paul speaks of covenant, it is always in the plural: "They are Israelites, and to them belong the adoption, the covenants, the giving of the law, the worship, and the promises";[44] "Remember that you were at that time separated from Christ, alienated from the commonwealth of Israel and strangers to the covenants of promise, having no hope and without God in the world."[45] Theological categories, such as the covenant of grace, can indeed be helpful—if they conform to the biblical record. But where Scripture does not fit the category, we must adjust the latter to the former.

We can also say that the New Testament treats such a suggestion of the moral law as trans-covenantal and given to Adam as an anachronism. Paul draws a distinction; an unfolding that recognizes the era before law, and the one after it: "For sin was

41. Wellum, "Baptism," 116.
42. Wellum, "Baptism," 127.
43. 1 Cor 5:7.
44. Rom 9:4.
45. Eph 2:12.

indeed in the world before the law was given."[46] If Adam was given the moral law in his innocence, it makes no sense that sin was in the world before the law was given. What sin would there have been that preceded the fall of humanity? The order Paul gives is first sin, then the law. One may protest that Paul frequently refers to the Mosaic law, rather than the overarching moral law, using the terms synonymously, and this is what he does here in Romans 5. Indeed he does, because the apostle knew only a single category of "law." This demonstrates that the Mosaic law (or moral law) was not given to Adam.

This is also the thrust of Paul's argument in Galatians 3: "This is what I mean: the law, which came 430 years afterward, does not annul a covenant previously ratified, so as to make the promise void."[47] Here, too, Paul locates the advent of the law not with Adam in the Garden, but rather at Sinai. In contrasting law and promise, Paul rejects the law as having any place in the covenant with Abraham.

Many have argued that it is specifically and only for justification that Paul disavows any role for the law: "For if the inheritance comes by the law, it no longer comes by promise."[48] The apostle certainly affirms this, but it is nowhere in his doctrine that our relationship to the law for justification is severed, but for sanctification, it remains. Andrew Wakefield rightly asks, "If Christians can and should keep the law once they are enabled by the Spirit, why is Paul so concerned if the Galatians—who are already believers, who have already received the Spirit (Gal. 3:2-5)—take up the law?"[49] Such a view makes a major argument of the Galatian epistle superfluous. It is an "unlawful" use of the law to divide it in this way.

Paul's further argument in Galatians 3 is an answer to the questions (similar to the one asked rhetorically at the end of Roman 3), "why then the law?" and "Is the law then contrary to the promises of God?" The illustration of the law as our pedagogue,

46. Rom. 5:13.
47. Gal 3:17.
48. Gal 3:18.
49. Wakefield, *Where to Live*, 201.

our guardian (this will be further discussed later), only makes sense if seen in the course of salvation history. Now that faith has come, we are no longer under a guardian. We have, as it were, reached the age of majority, and thus the previous captivity has ended. The covenantal change that occurred with the cross has completely altered what had prevailed in the prior age. If we assign a role to the Ten Commandments as binding upon believers of all ages, we fail to properly distinguish God's covenantal dealings with his people in previous ages, nor do we give appropriate place to the new covenant as being truly new. Asked differently, if believers are still under the pedagogue, has the faith Paul speaks of in fact arrived?

John Murray makes a similar argument for covenantal continuity. He seeks to show that, throughout the Old Testament, the covenants were the same; specifically, the Abrahamic covenant and the Mosaic covenant. If a common thread of grace runs through both of these, then it is not unthinkable that the new covenant contains elements of law, or that the Decalogue itself remains.

> The Mosaic covenant in respect of this condition of obedience is not in a different category from the Abrahamic. 'And God said to Abraham, "Thou shalt keep my covenant, therefore, thou, and thy seed after thee in their generations."' (Genesis 17:9). Of Abraham God said, "For I know him, that he will command his children and his household after him, and they shall keep the way of the Lord, to do justice and judgment; that the Lord may bring upon Abraham that which he hath spoken of him." (Genesis 18:19). There is nothing principally different in the necessity of keeping the covenant and of obeying God's voice, characteristic of the Mosaic covenant, from what is involved in the keeping of the covenant required in the Abrahamic.

> The holiness which is demanded by the covenant fellowship [of the Mosaic covenant] is expressed concretely in obedience to the divine commandments. This is really all that needs to be said to demonstrate not only the *consonance* of the demand for obedience with the covenant

> as one of religious relationship on the highest level of
> spirituality but also the *necessity* of such a demand. It is
> because the covenant is one of union and communion
> with God that the condition of obedience is demanded.[50]

But the differences between the Abrahamic and Mosaic covenants are profound. Paul is careful to contrast these two in their basis, their blessings, and their duration. The Abrahamic covenant rests on faith, apart from works. The Mosaic covenant demands obedience to the written code. The Abrahamic covenant extends to all nations and peoples, but God made the Mosaic covenant with the nation of Israel only. The Abrahamic covenant is overarching in its scope. It both predates the Mosaic and remains after the Mosaic is brought to an end. In 2 Corinthians 3:11, Paul refers to the end of Mosaic covenant, but he points to the gospel fulfilling elements of the Abrahamic covenant and its promises.

Murray is choosing his references carefully, but the whole context cannot support his conclusion. God's dealings with Abraham did not start in chapter 17, but rather in chapter 12 when he was called out of Ur of the Chaldees. In the subsequent chapters, God makes promises to Abraham, to give the land to him and his offspring, to bless him, to make him a father of a multitude. These promises are unconditional. God attaches no caveats or probation whatsoever to what he tells Abraham. Abraham's faith in God's promise is counted to him for righteousness. The covenant is ratified in chapter 15, with God again doing all of it.

When we come to chapter 17, which Murray quotes, earlier in the chapter God has said: "Behold, my covenant is with you, and you shall be the father of a multitude of nations."[51] The statements at verse 9 refer specifically to circumcision, which is not a new covenant, different from what God had already ratified with Abraham, but rather a sign of this unconditional covenant. Paul confirms this in Romans when he says of Abraham, "He received the sign of circumcision as a seal of the righteousness that he had by faith while he was still uncircumcised. The purpose was to

50. Murray, *Principles of Conduct*, 197, 198.
51. Gen 17:4.

make him the father of all who believe without being circumcised, so that righteousness would be counted to them as well."[52]

What Murray avers to be happening here is that God enjoins obedience upon Abraham as a condition of a covenant that he is instituting, but this reading is inaccurate. The covenant was already in place; Abraham's relationship with God was by faith, not through obeying commands. Circumcision is no new covenant with Abraham, but an *ex post facto* seal of what God had already put in place. Even those of the same confessional tradition as Murray have pointed out the problems with this position. In an essay addressing just this question, T. David Gordon identifies at least five significant differences between the Abrahamic and Mosaic covenants, including that fact that "The Abrahamic covenant is characterized by faith; the Sinai covenant is characterized by works of the law."[53] In Galatians chapter 3, the contrasts between these two covenants are vast. Gordon further comments,

> "Many are uncomfortable with such contrasts, fearing that they are implicitly Lutheran (or worse, dispensationalist). In an effort to diminish these unwelcome contrasts, many in the Reformed tradition have dismissed the contrasts by suggesting that what Paul is contrasting is some first-century legalistic abuse of the Sinai covenant to the Abrahamic covenant, not the two covenant-administrations themselves. The evidence of the text will not support such evasive action, however. When he illustrated the matter in [Galatians] chapter 4, for instance, citing Sarah and Hagar, he did not say that these two women were figuratively two ways of understanding the covenant, one right and one wrong. Rather he said, 'these two women are two covenants [αὗται γάρ εἰσιν δύο διαθῆκαι]. One is from Mount Sinai, bearing children for slavery; she is Hagar' (Gal. 4:24)."[54]

That slavery is due to the law, and obligation to it is characteristic of the Mosaic covenant, not the Abrahamic.

52. Rom 4:11.
53. Gordon, "Abraham and Sinai," 246.
54. Gordon, "Abraham and Sinai," 250–51.

Obedience to God's commands was there prior to the law given at Sinai. Adam did not obey, but the substance of his disobedience was not breaching the moral law or the Ten Commandments. He did not obey God's command not to eat of the tree. What God gave prior to Sinai was not the Ten Commandments. Despite confessional documents, there is no Scriptural support for placing the moral law in Eden. Rather, there is specific biblical evidence for law coming 430 years after the promise, and its obligation coming to an end with the advent of the new covenant. Much of the law debate and the insistence that it remains a rule of life for Christians hinge on this point: there are really not two covenants, but one overarching covenant of grace. The apostolic statements run counter to this, however. Both in 2 Corinthians and in Galatians, Paul is clear to make a contrast between the Sinai covenant and the new covenant, and to say that the law as obligation belongs only to Sinai.

Are Gentiles under the Law?

If there is not a biblical case for the Mosaic law outside the boundaries of the Mosaic covenant, is there a case for it outside the boundaries of ethnic Israel? That is, are gentiles under the law? Throughout the Old Testament, one can distinguish between the terms nation and nations, people and peoples. The former refers to Israel, while the latter refers to the gentiles: "Why do the nations rage, and the peoples plot in vain?"[55] David asks. And in the verse from Psalm 147 previously noted, David states that God has not given his laws to other nations. In this sense, then, God has given the law to Israel. But the question is not without complication.

In the great legal brief that is the book of Romans, Paul spends the first 3 chapters laying out a case for the just judgment of God upon mankind who have spurned him—Jew and gentile. If we ask who the subjects of law are, Paul answers, "whatever the law speaks, it speaks to those who are under law, so that every

55. Ps 2:1.

mouth may be stopped, and the whole world may be accountable to God." (Rom 3:19). Paul is referring to the Jewish nation with his reference to those under law. But what of the gentiles—did the law of Moses bind them? The majority of commentators on Romans do not see that God has placed the gentiles under the law. One of Paul's purposes in these early chapters is to establish the universality of guilt for all mankind. Because of that, there will be universality of judgment as well. All who sin will come under judgment. But this does not mean that God will use the same revealed law to judge all mankind.

W. H. Griffith-Thomas comments, "The standard for the Jew will be the law of Moses, but the standard for the Gentile will be the law of conscience. The Apostle means by 'sin without the law' and 'perish without the law' that they will perish by unfaithfulness to a law which they possess, namely, the law of nature; not to a law which they have never heard, namely, the law of Moses."[56]

If there is any law that the gentiles are under, it is the law of conscience. We might as readily term this the principle of conscience, and others have called it natural law.[57] That is, these things are innately known by humans, and thus are universal. This was one of the central themes in Luther's understanding of the Decalogue. A principal reason he continued to preach it was because he believed it accorded with natural law: "I keep the commandments which Moses has given, not because Moses gave commandment, but because they have been implanted in me by nature, and Moses agrees exactly with nature, etc."[58] But Luther likewise dismissed some of what Moses wrote, even parts of the Decalogue that he be-

---

56. Griffith-Thomas, *Romans*, 80.

57. Michael F. Bird argues for yet another view, that the gentiles here spoken of are in fact gentile believers: "Paul is not talking about Gentiles who have a *natural law* inscribed in their hearts. Instead he is talking about some Gentiles who do not have access to the law as intrinsic to their ethnic identity, or birth, and yet have the works of the law inscribed on their hearts . . . This 'inward Jew,' who is circumcised in his heart by the Spirit, is a Gentile Christian" (Bird, *Romans*, 78–79). If Bird's view is correct, it does not alter the fact that gentiles are not under the Mosaic law.

58. "How Christians Should Regard Moses" (1525), in *LW* 34:168.

lieved did not accord with what all men know. For example, he did not believe the Sabbath day to be one of those implanted by nature.

Luther is not alone in questioning the boundaries of natural law. Christopher Seitz believes several of the Ten Commandments are not knowable outside of the explicit revelation of God.

> Not knowable apart from positive law, that is, law as commanded, in this case, by the God of Israel, at Sinai. That especially the first four commandments, which deal with the revealed name and identity of God as personally disclosed to Israel, cannot be written off nature ought to be self-evident. If we think these are natural laws, we have probably not just misheard them, but domesticated them as well.[59]

The tenth commandment may fit into Seitz's category as well, for Paul says that he didn't know what coveting was until the law told him. In other words, the prohibition on it doesn't seem to be embedded in the conscience; at least Paul ascribes his understanding of it to the revealed law at Sinai.

The idea of natural law again brings us back to the law as a principle. When applied to human hearts—not just to Jewish hearts—a law, a regulation, will have a predictable effect. It will in one sense induce what it prohibits. A few years ago, I had an ear condition that required an injection, followed by a period of lying on my side while the medication took effect. On his way out the door, the doctor said: "Oh, and try not to swallow for the next twenty minutes or so." That, of course, made me focus almost single-mindedly on swallowing, which I did more times than I otherwise would have.

In the sense of widely applicable principle, then, we can speak of gentiles being under law. Westerholm notes that, because Paul has consigned all humanity as guilty before God, "It seems that Paul, speaking somewhat loosely, allows that Gentiles delivered from God's wrath against sinners (Rom 1:18; 5:9; 1 Thess 1:10;

---

59. Seitz, "Ten Commandments," 21.

etc.) are delivered from the (analogous) 'curse of the law' in Gal 3:13."[60] Schreiner concurs:

> it is more likely that the "we" who receive adoption in Galatians 4:5 refers to both Jews and Gentiles. Otherwise, Paul would be undercutting one of the central themes of Galatians—both Jews and Gentiles are adopted as sons. So, there is a sense in which he places the Gentiles under the law here, probably because they lived under the dominion of sin.[61]

Gentiles, too, are under the dominion of sin, and therefore the law would do its work of condemning them as well. Their thoughts accuse (i.e., condemn) them, because what they know to be right, they do not perform; and what they know to be wrong, they do nonetheless. In this sense, one could speak of gentiles being under law.

But Paul does not say that gentiles have the law of Moses written on their hearts. He argues for a knowledge of good and evil that is discernible apart from the Sinai revelation, but such knowledge is neither equal to nor as full as the law given at Sinai. Nevertheless, it is sufficient to justly condemn those who act contrary to that knowledge. At the start of Romans, he has similarly argued that gentiles are without excuse regarding God's existence and the worship owed him, due to the witness of nature as testimony to God's power and divinity. But this, too, is not equal to the Mosaic law. As Seitz notes, it is difficult to see how conscience alone would inform gentiles of something such as "Thou shalt not take the name of Jehovah thy God in vain."[62] Gentiles cannot have known the name of God, as revealed to Moses at the burning bush. Rather than the entire Decalogue, it is more likely that Paul is referencing only the second table of the law, the commandments governing behavior and interpersonal relationships, in equating this with the voice of conscience.

The verses prior to Romans 2:14, moreover, make the gentile position clear: "For all who have sinned *without the law* will

---

60. Westerholm, *Perspectives*, 303.

61. Schreiner, *40 Questions*, 79.

62. Exod 20:7, ASV.

also perish without the law."[63] The passage preempts any argument made by a Jew that his proximity to the law gives him an advantage when it comes to the judgment of God. God shows no partiality,[64] says Paul, but not because both Jew and gentile alike are under Mosaic law, but because God is a righteous judge: "For all who have sinned *without* the law will also perish without the law, and all who have sinned *under* the law will be judged by the law" (Rom 2:12; emphasis added). He draws the contrast between gentiles without law and Jews under law. It does not make sense to speak of those without law if all mankind is under the law of Moses.

To affirm that gentiles are under the Mosaic law, moreover, assumes that conditional statements Paul makes are indicative of the whole gentile world: "For when Gentiles, who do not have the law, by nature do what the law requires, they are a law to themselves, even though they do not have the law. They show that the work of the law is written on their hearts, while their conscience also bears witness, and their conflicting thoughts accuse or even excuse them" (Rom 2:14–15). Here, too, the apostle is drawing a distinction. He does not say that all gentiles behave this way; rather, he speaks of *when* they do the things that accord with the law. It is a conditional statement, to preclude any protest on the part of a Jew that they are superior to gentiles because they have the law. The statement, "even though they do not have the law," strengthens this argument. Whatever mankind knows as a result of conscience is not equal to having the law of Moses, that specific revelation given at Sinai to the descendants of Jacob alone. If it were the case that gentiles through conscience had an exact representation of the Mosaic law, then Jews would surely have this as well. They, too, have a conscience. There would be no further need for the revelation at Sinai if all mankind innately knows with the specificity of the Decalogue what God requires of them.

In the Ephesian epistle as well, Paul directly addresses the question of gentiles under law: "You Gentiles," he says "were strangers from the commonwealth of Israel," but the apostle says

63. Rom 2:12. Emphasis added.
64. Rom 2:11.

that God has made Jews and gentiles "both one and has broken down in his flesh the dividing wall of hostility by abolishing the law of commandments expressed in ordinances."[65] The law clearly represents a division between Jew and gentile, something that kept the two apart. While some commentators have said that the things Paul speaks about as abolished are the Jewish "boundary markers" (circumcision and the purity laws), that doesn't fit with Paul's overarching treatment of the law as a unit. The food laws and other purification laws separated Jews and gentiles, but Paul does not differentiate between parts of the law, saying gentiles are only released from the so-called ceremonial law. He always speaks of law as a whole in his epistles. And it is obvious that if the law separated Jew and gentile, it is because the gentile did not have and was not given the law.

A final incident to consider is the Jerusalem Council, recorded in Acts 15. The source of strife that required the council was the contention by some of the believing Pharisees regarding gentile converts: "It is necessary to circumcise them and to order them to keep the law of Moses."[66] The apostles and elders answered negatively to this demand. Peter replied, "why are you putting God to the test by placing a yoke on the neck of the disciples that neither our fathers nor we have been able to bear? But we believe that we will be saved through the grace of the Lord Jesus, just as they will."[67] After James speaks, the council agrees to a fourfold recommendation for gentile converts: abstain from the things polluted by idols, from sexual immorality, from what has been strangled, and from blood.

Some may claim that these are only ceremonial things, and not moral, but surely the first two items fit into the Decalogue—the moral law—even if the latter two belong to what many commonly think of as ceremonial, not at all part of the Ten Commandments. Why focus on these things and seemingly ignore the Sabbath, bearing false witness, or honoring parents? Could it be that

65. Eph 2:14.
66. Acts 15:5.
67. Acts 15:10–11.

the advice to the gentiles was situational? John Stott comments, "having established the principle that salvation is by grace alone through faith alone, without works, it was necessary to appeal to these Gentile believers to respect the consciences of their Jewish fellow-believers by abstaining from a few practices which might offend them."[68]

With this, Ben Witherington agrees, "The witness of Gentile Christians was important to James. They must not give Jews in the Diaspora the opportunity to complain that Gentile Christians were still practicing idolatry and immorality by going to pagan feasts even after beginning to follow Christ."[69] Paul himself will expand upon the importance of not causing brothers and sisters in Christ to stumble. Though they may have liberty to eat anything, they must behave with love toward fellow believers. Whatever conclusions we draw from the Jerusalem council, it is decidedly not a continuation of the Mosaic law, nor an imposition of it upon the gentile converts. To the question of whether or not gentiles should keep the law of Moses, the answer the council provides is to not trouble the gentiles with these things. The apostles and elders are happy to leave the law where they find it—among the Jews: "For from ancient generations Moses has had in every city those who proclaim him, for he is read every Sabbath in the synagogues."[70]

In a true sense, the question of whether gentiles were ever under the law is moot. The explicit statements of our death to the law,[71] that we are no longer under it,[72] and that the old covenant is obsolete[73] decide the matter. Paul's point in Romans was never to argue for gentile duty to the Mosaic law, but rather to contend for the universal guilt of both Jew and gentile. To claim a continuing obligation to law for gentile Christians is, moreover, superfluous. In Christ there is neither Jew nor gentile. Those saved by God's

68. Stott, *Acts*, 248.

69. Witherington, *Acts*, 463.

70. Acts 15:21.

71. Rom 7:4.

72. Rom 7:14.

73. 2 Cor 3:11.

grace are on an equal footing before him. Ethnic identity is not a factor in how we relate to God, how we live before him, nor in how he relates to us. The question of whether gentiles were at one time the subjects of law does not provide meaningful help in answering the question of the place of law within the church today.

The law given at Sinai was the covenant treaty between God and Israel—the descendants of Jacob. The nations, gentiles, did not receive the law, and were not entrusted with the "oracles of God."[74] While it is convenient to group the commandments of the Mosaic law into traditional categories of moral, civil, and ceremonial, this can obscure the way the New Testament regards the law as a whole. Moreover, by extracting just one category of "moral law," and claiming a continuing obligation to it for believers of all ages, we disregard the unfolding of God's plan, and of his purpose for law in salvation history.

74. Rom 3:2.

3

The Purpose of Law in Salvation History

In some ways "the love of Christ" not only redefines the law but also sees the incarnate, crucified Christ as the divine expression, and thus replacement, of the law.

—Gordon Fee[1]

God's Unfolding Revelation

THE CONCEPT OF SALVATION history is the unfolding of God's redemptive plan throughout biblical revelation. This is both linear and progressive. Truths introduced in the earlier books of Scripture are subsequently developed, expanding and building on the foundation. At the burning bush, God tells Moses, "I appeared unto Abraham, unto Isaac, and unto Jacob, as God Almighty; but by my name Jehovah I was not known to them."[2] God was revealing something to Moses not previously known. Similarly, when we come to Romans, Paul speaks about God exercising forbearance in passing over the sins previously committed. And the reason God

---

1. Fee, *Pauline Christianity*, 231–32.
2. Exod 3:6, ASV.

did so "was to show his righteousness at the present time."[3] What is different about the present time, as Paul speaks, is that Jesus had come to earth, suffered and died on the cross, and risen again. God had set him forth, presenting him as a propitiation for our sins. He, through his death, reconciled us to God. That did not happen in prior ages, for at a point in time, Jesus was born, took on human flesh, and died in our place. Paul speaks of this to the Galatians when he says, "when the fullness of time had come, God sent forth his son."[4] All of these examples demonstrate that God was doing something new, something he had indeed foreshadowed and typified in prior ages, but the manifestation of it had only come at this point in time.

These are developments in salvation history, and they show that, with the progress of revelation, some things are replaced and superseded. The Levitical offerings pointed to Christ, but when the one to whom they pointed arrived, these sacrifices became obsolete. In the epistle to the Hebrews, the word "better" occurs repeatedly, as a demonstration of just such developments. We now have better promises, a better covenant, and better sacrifices. Hebrews is the book where we can clearly see that the new covenant is not only temporally newer than the old, but also qualitatively superior.

This qualitative superiority does not imply flaws in God's previous dealings with mankind. But it does mean that the fullness of God's message is embodied in the Lord Jesus Christ, and that with his life, ministry, death, and resurrection, salvation history reaches an apex that defines who God's people are and how they are to live. The prior eras anticipated this completeness and pointed forward to this "fullness of time" of God manifest in the flesh. Included in the apostolic message is that the law belongs to these previous ages, rather than the present era of salvation history.

The Decalogue is the treaty document between the nation of Israel and God. "And he declared to you his covenant, which he commanded you to perform, that is, the Ten Commandments."[5]

3. Rom 3:26.
4. Gal 4:4.
5. Deut 4:13.

Its provenance is with Israel and the exodus from Egypt, and was a treaty with a time limitation. Paul demonstrates this in several passages. In 2 Corinthians 3, he says that "what once had glory has come to have no glory at all, because of the glory that surpasses it. For if what was being brought to an end came with glory, much more will what is permanent have glory."[6] Paul sets up a series of propositional statements that he then affirms. We could also read his introduction of each proposition with an "if" as "since," for he predicates these affirmations not on the first part possibly being true, but being true in fact. It is true that the ministry of death, carved in letters of stone, came with glory; therefore, does it not follow that the ministry of the Spirit has even more glory? If the ministry of condemnation had glory, will not the ministry of righteousness exceed it? Paul asks questions that he knows his readers will undoubtedly answer with "yes!" The apostle contrasts the old covenant with the new. To the old covenant belong death (v. 7), condemnation (v. 9), and fading glory (v. 10). To the new covenant belong the Spirit (v. 8), righteousness (v. 9), and surpassing glory (v. 10). "Each comparison is designed to show both that the new era of the Spirit is more glorious than the era of the Mosaic law and that the era of the Mosaic law is passing away."[7] We often think of what is etched in stone as being permanent, but here Paul says the opposite, that the commandments in stone are brought to an end. One cannot assert that Paul claims abrogation only for the ceremonial or civil portions of the law while the Ten Commandments retain their obligation, since it was the Decalogue that God carved in stone at Sinai—yet Paul calls it impermanent. Indeed, the very adjectives of "old" and "new" speak to a setting aside of the former, and continuation of the latter.

The other passages that similarly speak of the old covenant as temporary are in Hebrews 8: "But as it is, Christ has obtained a ministry that is as much more excellent than the old as the covenant he mediates is better, since it is enacted on better promises. For if that first covenant had been faultless, there would have been

---

6. 1 Cor 3:10–11.

7. Thielman, *Paul & the Law*, 112.

no occasion to look for a second."[8] Here, too, the writer contrasts old and new; the old was not without fault, and therefore a new covenant replacing the old was brought in. Later in the chapter, he states, "In speaking of a new covenant, he makes the first one obsolete."[9] The message is clear that the old is set aside, succeeded by a new, better covenant.

One of the fuller presentations on the law's purpose is in Galatians 3, and through his argument Paul has much to say about salvation history. In verses 19–25 he presents answers to the primary question, "Why then the law?" It was added "because of transgressions," he says. One view of what Paul says is that the law's purpose is to actually increase sin, for the purposes of driving the despondent sinner to Christ. In support of this is what Paul wrote in Romans 5:20: "Now the law came in to increase the trespass." Schreiner believes this provoking function to be the primary one: "Both the context of Galatians and the parallel with Romans 5:20 suggest that Paul teaches that the law was given *to cause sin*."[10]

Others think that, by the phrase "because of transgressions," Paul means the law came in to control sin, and to act as a restraint. The ordinances God gave them preserved Israel from the sins of the surrounding nations—provided they kept them. Repeatedly, God told Israel he was casting out the nations because they had polluted the land by their sin: "Do not make yourselves unclean by any of these things, for by all these the nations I am driving out before you have become unclean."[11] While this may have been one function of law under the old covenant, the surrounding language in Galatians argues against it being the primary one. Israel's history, too, demonstrates that it was plainly ineffective in performing this function.

Whatever restraining function the law may have had, Paul doesn't portray this positively. He says "we were held captive under

8. Heb 8:6–7.

9. Heb 8:13.

10. Schreiner, *Law and Its Fulfillment*, 75.

11. Lev 18:24.

the law, imprisoned until the coming faith would be revealed."[12] The apostle's comparison in subsequent verses of the law to a guardian or pedagogue leads some to conclude that it was our teacher, bringing us to Christ. The King James Version's unfortunate rendering of this as "schoolmaster" gave this sense. But the pedagogue was not a benevolent tutor, as one may think: "These pedagogues had the bad image of being rude, rough, and good for no other business . . . the figure of the pedagogue is looked upon as a hard but necessary instrument in bringing a person to achieve and realize virtue."[13] "Their name, consequently, had a stigma attached to it."[14] If the law performs a function of training, or of leading one to Christ, why would Paul speak negatively about it, using the words "imprisoned" and "captive"? Martyn likewise doubts Paul's intention to present the law as our teacher. The law "is not a pedagogical guide, but an imprisoning warden," he says, in that "six of the ten times Paul refers to humans being 'under the power of' the *paidagogos*, he identifies that enslaving power as the Law."[15] Moreover, if the law had such a teaching function, Paul would not have considered it limited to a certain time in history. Das puts it this way: "If the pedagogue were fulfilling a positive educational function in leading people to Christ, it would be unclear why Paul would consider the pedagogy to have ended with Christ's coming."[16]

In both Romans and Galatians, Paul assigns an enslaving power to the law, but it is a captivity that has ended with the coming of Christ. The eschatological purpose of the law has been completed. As he did in Second Corinthians, Paul presents a picture of before and after—the period of law and the age of the promised seed, Christ. Rule-of-life theologians acknowledge this, as Calvin says: "He had undertaken to prove two things: that the law

---

12. Gal 3:23.

13. Betz, *Galatians*, 177.

14. Ridderbos, *Galatia*, 146.

15. Martyn, *Galatians*, 363.

16. Das, *Galatians*, 375.

is a preparation for Christ, and that it is temporary."[17] But Calvin wants to preserve a pedagogical use for the law, and asks,

> But here again it may be asked whether the law is so abolished that it has nothing to do with us. I reply that the law, so far as it is a rule of life, is a bridle which keeps us in the fear of the Lord, a spur to correct the slackness of our flesh, in short, so far as it is profitable for teaching, correcting, reproving, that believers may be instructed in every good work, is as much in force as ever, and remains intact.[18]

This is but another way of stating that the law has no role in justification, but it remains a standard for believers for sanctification. I will discuss good works later, but while doing good is important to Paul, he does not use the law to define for Christians what that good is.

Calvin doesn't draw this conclusion that the law remains a rule of life from the biblical text, but from his conviction that the pedagogical function remains in place. Paul has disavowed the law as a rule of life for the Christian, assigning it squarely to the prior age: "But now that faith has come, we are no longer under a guardian."[19] The portion of Scripture Calvin alludes to in 2 Timothy 3:16 is sufficiently broad to say that Paul refers to the entire Old Testament. It is not at all clear that Paul means the commandments of Moses in what he writes to Timothy.

Indeed, in Romans Paul presents the opposite of what Calvin affirms. The law, Paul teaches, arouses our sinful flesh, rather than correcting the slackness of it. His view is not modified even after the coming of Christ. The law was not contrary to God's purposes, but it pointed forward to the time of its own end, a time when the promised seed should come: "The law was our guardian until Christ came," he says, but now that the seed of Abraham—Christ—has come, this eschatological purpose of the law has been fulfilled.

17. Calvin, *Galatians*, 67.
18. Calvin, *Galatians*, 67.
19. Gal 3:25.

The law points the way to its own successor, to Christ himself as the fulfillment of all its types and shadows.

Adam and Christ: The Importance of Headship

At several junctures in his letters, Paul expounds upon the changed identity of believers. For the apostle, the idea of being "in Christ" means a radically new position for the Christian, something unknown to previous eras of salvation history. When God justifies a person who believes in Jesus, this change of identity occurs. But prior to that, each of us had a different identity as a child of Adam. All of humankind experiences the disastrous effects of being part of Adam's progeny. In chapter 5 of Romans, Paul sets forth Adam as the representative of humanity—as our "federal head." At 5:12, he says that sin came into the world through one man, and death through sin, and so death spread to all men because all sinned. When he sinned in the garden, he did so representatively, for all of humanity was yet in him when he sinned. Further into the chapter, in verses 18–19, the apostle refers to one trespass that led to universal condemnation, and by one man's disobedience, the many were made sinners.

These passages are not without their challenges. Does Paul mean to say that Adam's sin is credited to us because he acted on our behalf, or does he say that each of us sins, like Adam, because of the nature we inherited from him? Moo refers to the tension of these passages and says "Paul in v. 12 asserts that all people die because they sin on their own account; and in vv. 18–19 he claims that they die because of Adam's sin. Paul does not resolve these two perspectives; and we do wrong to try to force a resolution that Paul himself never made."[20] Indeed, resolving this question is not necessary to see that Paul teaches headship in the fifth chapter of Romans. Verse 17 demonstrates this as well, where Paul says "death reigned through that one man." Paul is assigning to Adam a position of headship. Robert C. Tannehill expands on this: "Through

---

20. Moo, *Romans*, 324.

Adam's transgression the reign of death was established (v. 17). Christ's 'righteous act' has similar significance (cf. vs. 18–19, 21). These two acts are the founding acts of the two dominions."[21]

As Tannehill also points out, Jesus acted representatively when he died on the cross. His death on the cross was the founding act of the church. All that is ours as believers comes to us because he is our head: "Much more will those who receive the abundance of grace and the free gift of righteousness reign in life through the one man Jesus Christ";[22] "For as by a man came death, by a man has come also the resurrection from the dead."[23] This is also why Jesus is called the second Adam and the last Adam in 1 Corinthians. Even as Adam was the head of a race of sinful humanity, so also is Christ the head of justified believers. To be in Christ is to be reckoned as part of redeemed humanity, no longer counted among the condemned humanity in Adam. And a key point is that Scripture presses the claim of obligation to law upon the Adamic man.

If Romans 5 is the explanation of the two federal heads (and all mankind must be under one of these two), then chapter 6 presents the reign of sin and death, and how we get free of it. But before Paul explains our freedom from sin and death, he explains our captivity to it: "We know that our old self was crucified with him in order that the body of sin might be brought to nothing, so that we would no longer be enslaved to sin."[24] The word translated "self" is *anthropos*, most often rendered "man," or as the KJV has it, "our old man."

There is contention about what the old man designates, chiefly over the question of whether an "old man" and "new man" coexist in the Christian. John MacArthur affirms, "Biblical terminology, then, does not say that a Christian has two different natures. He has but one nature, the new nature in Christ. The old self dies, and the new self lives. They do not coexist."[25] This is largely a

---

21. Tannehill, *Dying and Rising*, 27.

22. Rom 5:17.

23. 1 Cor 15:22.

24. Rom 6:6.

25. MacArthur, *Ephesians*, 164.

semantic disagreement, because no one affirms that the believer is now without sin, or is not subject to temptation. No matter what we call it, there is that within the Christian that can still respond to sin. Moule's paraphrase is helpful: "This knowing, that our old man, as out of Christ and under Adam's headship, under guilt and in moral bondage, was crucified with Christ."[26] Wuest comments also, "Thus, the old man here refers to that person the believer was before he was saved, totally depraved, unregenerate, lacking the life of God."[27] Dunn, too, calls it "the condition of life prior to conversion . . . explicitly life under the age prior to Christ, the old covenant . . . man belonging to the age of Adam, dominated by sin and death."[28] Finally, Godet says, "The expression: our old man, denotes human nature such as it has been made by the sin of him in whom it was originally concentrated, fallen Adam."[29] Whether we see this expression as old nature, old man, or sinful nature is less the point than what Paul means to convey, and that is, as Moo phrases it, "a realm transfer."[30]

This is like emigration from one country to another. When a person leaves their country of birth and takes citizenship in a new country, from that point on, their new home defines their new citizenship. They carry a passport from the new country, and other governments treat them as citizens of their new homeland. It would make no sense for them to continue adhering to the laws of their birth country while living in the new land. Nor would their new nation recognize those statues as valid. This is a byproduct of gaining citizenship in the new land. They've undergone a realm transfer, and that's the same sort of thing that happens to someone who believes in Jesus. He or she gets a new spiritual passport. That passport precludes any obligation to the old covenant. The obligations of the new aren't at odds with the old, but they exceed them.

26. Moule, *Romans*, 101.

27. Wuest, *Romans*, 101.

28. Dunn, *Romans*, 318.

29. Godet, *Romans*, 415.

30. Moo, *Romans*, 354.

Our old nature, the Adamic, is what responds to law, rather than the second man, the heavenly. This is not to say that the law was given to Adam in the garden. Rather, it is a contrast with the new creation in Christ. The law was given to Israel, not to gentiles, but there is another way of looking at the law's intent and subjects. One can say that the law has both a covenantal home (Israel) and a spiritual object (the Adamic man.) When Paul describes the condemnation of the law in Romans 7, he is not describing something that Jews alone would experience. When the law is applied to any human heart, it will induce what it forbids. That provocation to sin arises from the Adamic nature within us. The new nature may agree that the law is holy and good, but we are still subject to the temptations of sin. The born-again believer therefore focuses not on the earthly, because our resurrected and risen identity does not rely on the law for conformity to Christ. We walk by the Spirit, not by the law.

We who were in Adam have been crucified with Christ, and we are no longer bound to that nature. This is consistent with the apostle's teaching elsewhere. He tells the Colossians that God has "delivered us out of the power of darkness, and translated us into the kingdom of the Son of his love."[31] To the Corinthians he also presents the headship of the two Adams: "Thus it is written, 'The first man Adam became a living being'; the last Adam became a life-giving spirit."[32] And Paul also makes clear that believers belong to the last Adam: "Just as we have borne the image of the man of dust, we shall also bear the image of the heavenly."[33] This comparison of the earthly and the heavenly accords with what he tells the Colossians later in the epistle: "If then you have been raised with Christ, seek the things that are above, where Christ is, seated at the right hand of God. Set your minds on things that are above, not on things that are on earth. For you have died, and your life is hidden with Christ in God."[34] All of these point to our

31. Col 1:13, ASV.
32. 1 Cor 15:45.
33. 1 Cor 15:49.
34. Col 3:1–3.

new identity in Christ, as raised with him, and joined to his resurrection life. However Scripture may describe the redeemed of prior ages—Abraham, the friend of God, or David, the man after God's own heart—it does not speak of them having been raised up and seated with Christ in the heavenly places. That is a uniquely Christian position.

But it is clear that the death we experienced is judicial rather than actual. Turner comments, "The fact is that, for Paul, believers also continue to share solidarity with Adam—until the resurrection (1 Cor 15:49). Before that, their lives are still lived in what Paul can call a 'body of death' (Rom 8:10, 13). Death, the fruit of humanity's solidarity with sin in Adam, is still Christian experience too."[35] We are subject to the effects of sin, and its corruption. In Adam we all die. Even though we have this inheritance from our first father, this does not mean we must continue to live under the mastery of sin. This is the reason for Paul's insistence that those in Christ have died with him and are associated with him in his death "so that the body of sin might be brought to nothing, so that we would no longer be enslaved to sin."[36] Is Paul equating the body with sin? Leon Morris considers this untenable: "We may reject without hesitation the view that it means that the body is inherently sinful and that it is the source of sin. This is not a New Testament view and Paul never gives it countenance . . . On the whole it seems that Paul is here referring to the physical body which so easily responds to sinful impulses."[37] The body, then, weakened by our Adamic union, is often the locus of sin. We carry out and perform sin in our bodies. To be sure, we can sin with our minds alone, but all too frequently our sin will manifest itself through our bodies. As Boice says, "although I am not ultimately my body, I am nevertheless so much formed by it that I cannot escape its influences."[38]

---

35. Turner, *Holy Spirit*, 127.

36. Rom 6:6.

37. Morris, *Romans*, 251, 252.

38. Boice, *Romans*, 668.

One of the most definitive statements about the law occurs in Romans 7 and contains an illustration of a married woman who becomes a widow: "Or do you not know, brothers—for I am speaking to those who know the law—that the law is binding on a person only as long as he lives? For a married woman is bound by law to her husband while he lives, but if her husband dies she is released from the law of marriage. Accordingly, she will be called an adulteress if she lives with another man while her husband is alive. But if her husband dies, she is free from that law, and if she marries another man she is not an adulteress. Likewise, my brothers, you also have died to the law through the body of Christ, so that you may belong to another, to him who has been raised from the dead, in order that we may bear fruit for God."[39]

Commentators have sometimes shaken their heads over this passage because it seems like Paul has spoiled the illustration. He begins by saying "if her husband dies" (and the law is the husband in his picture), but then switches to "you also have died"—and says we are married to another. How can one who is dead be married again? This is looking at particulars too intently, rather than the overarching point the apostle wishes to make, which is simply that death severs the obligation to law. Believers are those who have died—and been raised up. Our faith in Christ means a new creation, justification, redemption, and a new identity.

Because of our new identity as joined to the risen Christ, the old relationship to law has ended. We have died to the law and now belong to another, even the risen Christ. Furnish comments that "The point here is evident: the Christian, like the widow, stands in an entirely new relationship to the law; he is no longer under its jurisdiction (ὑπὸ νόμον), [Rom] 6:14-15). Because in Christ's death he has died to the law (v. 4a), it is no longer binding on him (cf. v. 1b)."[40] It is easy to see that this is true even in the laws of human government. If a person is found guilty of murder, sentenced to death, and that sentence is carried out, it is not possible for the law to have any further claim on that person. He is dead. "Likewise

39. Rom 7:1–4.
40. Furnish, *Theology and Ethics*, 177.

my brothers, you also have died to the law through the body of Christ." Christians are those who have undergone such a sentence, albeit in Christ. We are those who have been united with him in a death like his.[41] Our union with Christ, our identification with him in his resurrection, means the old relationship to law, and any continual claim it can have on us, is gone.

Some have tried to mitigate Paul's statement here, to qualify and soften it, to say that he is not speaking of all law, but only a part. Calvin is quick to caution his readers of this.

> We must keep in mind that Paul is referring here only to that part of the law which is proper to the ministry of Moses. We must never imagine that the law is in any way abrogated in regard to the Ten Commandments, in which God has taught us what is right and has ordered our life, because the will of God must stand for ever[sic].[42]

Paul doesn't teach this division in the law that Calvin claims. In Paul's illustration, it is not some parts of the marriage obligation that end, but the whole of it. Shortly after this opening section of Romans 7, where he proclaims our death to the law, Paul will reference the tenth commandment (do not covet) contrary to Calvin's position that the Decalogue remains.

The goal of what Paul teaches here is freedom from the enslavement of sin. And the reason that he goes back to is this: "For one who has died has been set free from sin."[43] Death is what brings freedom to the believer. It is a death we died along with Christ, because of our union with him by faith. Baptism is the portrayal of that. This is how Paul began the sixth chapter, with the picture that believers were "buried therefore with him by baptism into death, in order that, just as Christ was raised from the dead by the glory of the Father, we too might walk in newness of life."[44]

---

41. Rom 6:5.
42. Calvin, *Romans*, 45.
43. Rom 6:7.
44. Rom 6:4.

Here, then, is the realm transfer that brings us under the headship of Christ, no longer bound to that of Adam. And what is vital to note is that the part law plays in this is to pass sentence, and to kill. It has no role in bringing or maintaining our life in Christ. When Scripture applies the law to mankind, it applies it to mankind in Adam, not to those in Christ. To be sure, Paul has a deep interest in the spiritual lives and growth of his readers. Likeness to Christ, that sin might have an ever more distant connection to believers, is his desire for them. Accordingly, he writes, "Let not sin therefore reign in your mortal body, to make you obey its passions."[45] But how may we weaken that connection to sin? By not looking to the law to help us overcome sin in any way: "For sin will not have dominion over you, for you are not under law, but under grace."[46] Here is one of the apostle's clearest statements of contrast between law and grace. Paul never says we die to sin in order to keep the law; rather, when we die to sin, we die to the law also.

It is difficult to see how being under obligation to law can at all be "of use to the regenerate, to restrain their corruptions,"[47] since Paul avows that the commandments themselves stir up corruption in us. They do so "because the mind of the flesh is enmity with God, for it is not subject to the law of God, neither indeed can it be."[48] Contrary to any suggestion that the law restrains corruption, Paul says it encourages sin. There is a way to victory over sin, but it is not through the law as a rule of life, not in this age of the Spirit.

The Law as Expression of God's Will

For many believers, God's will and the law are inextricably linked. Calvin's comments above demonstrate this belief that, since God is the same from eternity to eternity, and his moral norms do not

---

45. Rom 6:12.
46. Rom 6:14.
47. Westminster Assembly, *Confession of Faith*, 19:5,6.
48. Rom 8:7, ASV.

change, then it is not possible that our obligation to his law ends, in that it is the expression of his moral will. Willem A. VanGemeren writes,

> God gave them [Adam and Eve] ordinances (creation ordinances) that are perpetually binding on all human beings. The creation ordinances regulate rest, patterned after God's rest, establish responsible involvement (rule) over God's creation, and develop harmonious relationships with God, family members, and other human beings (Gen 1:28, 2:2–3, 24; cf. Eph 4:24) . . . The moral law in its written form does not contradict or change the will of God. Rather, it makes explicit and amplifies that will as originally expressed in natural law. Since the will of God does not change, the law remains virtually the same throughout redemptive history.[49]

But VanGemeren reads too much into what God gave to Adam prior to the fall. There is no command to Adam and Eve to rest. Rather, the text simply says that God blessed the seventh day and made it holy. VanGemeren makes the moral law part of creation, and since creation continues, though marred by sin, law continues as obligatory for believers. VanGemeren further says, since God himself is the one who established the moral law, we cannot say it does not retain its claim on us, for this would be saying that God retains no claim on us: "Creation-order and law-order are correlative. Law cannot be separated from the Lawgiver or from God's plan to bring order in creation. At Creation, God sent forth his word to create order. At Sinai, God sent forth this word to renew humans and prepare them for the new order."[50] VanGemeren's stance has much in common with the traditional Jewish view of the law: "In Early Judaism, it would have been inconceivable to restrict the law within temporal boundaries, since the law was known to be eternal in its glory and function."[51] But the believer's view of law must account for both testaments, not

49. VanGemeren, "Law," 18, 21.
50. VanGemeren, "Law," 24.
51. Longenecker, *Triumph of Abraham's God*, 118.

just one. The statements VanGemeren makes about the law as embedded in creation face the obstacle that the New Testament, and Paul specifically, never regard the law this way. Sinai prepares for the new order only by revealing and convicting mankind of sin, but the law itself is not part of the new order. It is to confuse the covenants to regard the law as embedded in creation.

In answer to the law remaining virtually the same throughout redemptive history, we might ask whether it is possible to separate the Creator from creation? Indeed, God is separate from his creation, and though he created all things and pronounced them good, he nevertheless destroyed all of it in the flood, preserving only Noah and his family through the ark. In other words, God brought an old order to an end, and began anew, though the previous order was his good handiwork. Here, too, the biblical text will not support such a reading as VanGemeren posits. He does not present anything other than Reformed confessional teaching. The *Westminster Larger Catechism* says that "the moral law is summarily comprehended in the Ten Commandments,"[52] but the scriptural basis for this is wanting. It demonstrates a common theme within rule-of-life adherents of finding in the law the perfect expression of God's will, or of seeing in the Decalogue the fullest pattern of holiness to which believers are to conform.

Calvin, too, assumes that the Ten Commandments represent the most refined expression of God's will for man: "They give this name [of moral law] specially to the first class, without which, true holiness of life and an immutable rule of conduct cannot exist . . . The moral law, then . . . is the true and eternal rule of righteousness prescribed to the men of all nations and of all times, who would frame their life agreeably to the will of God."[53] Guenter H. Haas observes,

> Because the law reveals the eternal will of God, it is, for Calvin, the ultimate moral norm. God alone has the authority to establish the rules and laws which govern people's lives. They cannot depart from the law without abandoning God himself. It presents his character and

52. Westminster, *Larger Catechism*, Q. 98.

53. Calvin, *Institutes*, 4.20.14–15.

reveals his perfect righteousness to them. If they would
be holy as God is holy, then they must submit to the law
as the perfect rule for the godly life.[54]

Here, too, Wesley joins Calvin: "The law of God (speaking after the
manner of men) is a copy of the eternal mind, a transcript of the
divine nature: Yea, it is the fairest offspring of the everlasting Father, the brightest efflux of his essential wisdom, the visible beauty
of the Most High."[55]

The New Testament doesn't present the law as an eternal rule
of righteousness, nor as the expression of God's character. Instead,
it puts forth the person of Christ as succeeding the law. John opens
his gospel by saying, "The law was given through Moses; grace and
truth came through Jesus Christ."[56] Believers in Jesus have a standard of holiness, but it is not found in the Decalogue. Indeed, Jesus'
own treatment of the law in the Sermon on the Mount demonstrates a standard beyond the law, and centered instead in his own
person and character. Does the law (the moral law, for that matter)
tell me to love my enemies? Jesus tells his followers to do so, not
because the law says so; indeed, he presents it as going beyond the
law. To love one another as he has loved us is grace surpassing the
law. The rule of conduct Jesus puts before the disciples is not an
immutable standard found in the Decalogue. Rather, it is a new
commandment, a standard not inscribed in stone, but found in the
character and person of the Lord Jesus himself. Luther recognized
this as well:

> If one of them had to be parted with, Christ, or the
> law, the law would have to be let go, not Christ. For if
> we have Christ, we can easily establish new laws and we
> shall judge all things rightly. Indeed, we would make new
> decalogues, as Paul does in all the epistles, and Peter, but
> above all Christ in the gospel. And those decalogues are
> clearer than the decalogue of Moses, just as the coun-
> tenance of Christ is brighter than the countenance of

54. Haas, "Calvin's Ethics," 97.
55. Wesley, *Use of the Law*, 309–10.
56. John 1:17.

> Moses. Nevertheless, since in the meantime we are inconstant in the spirit, and the flesh wars with the spirit, it is necessary, also on account of inconstant souls, to adhere to certain commands and writings of the apostles, lest the church be torn to pieces.[57]

Bruce Longenecker agrees that Paul's teaching presents a different understanding of whether the Mosaic law represents the highest expression of God's will: "According to Paul, Christ crucified is the embodiment of God's wisdom—the divine creative, sustaining and redemptive power. Claims of this sort fly in the face of the traditional view that the Torah and its stipulations were built into the very structures of the world. Instead of being eternal ordinances, Paul depicts Torah stipulations to be of a different order, being limited to the time between the giving of the law at Sinai and the coming of Christ."[58]

Brian Rosner's observations are worth noting here, because they navigate the scriptural evidence to show something other than law as the highest standard for Christians. He comments that, at least seven times in his epistles, Paul instructs his converts in God's will:

> All of these instances refer to Christians in relation to God's moral will. The point to note is that none of them indicates that Christians know God's will through the law. Two passages give concrete guidance concerning some specific aspect of God's will (1 Thess. 4:3: "It is God's will that you should be sanctified: that you should avoid sexual immorality"; NIV; and 1 Thess. 5:18: "give thanks in all circumstances, for this is God's will for you in Christ Jesus"). The only source indicated for this knowledge is that it is Paul's own instruction. Evidently, the Thessalonian believers know God's will through the authority of God's appointed messenger.[59]

---

57. *LW* 34:112–13.

58. Longenecker, *Triumph of Abraham's God*, 119.

59. Rosner, *Paul and the Law*, 91.

The apostle urges his converts to know God's will, and to conform to it. But the source of knowledge for believers in this age is not the Mosaic law. Hans Dieter Betz, commenting on Galatians, has stated it this way:

> For Paul, the will of God is not identical with and expressed by the Jewish Torah, which he understands in terms of his former Pharisaism (see [Gal] 5:3), but God's will is identical with the salvation in Christ (see [Gal] 1:4). The point about God's demands is that they are fulfilled—not that they 'rule'—and that fulfilled, they will be part of the salvation in Christ.[60]

The writer to the Hebrews acknowledges, "Long ago, at many times and in many ways, God spoke to our fathers by the prophets, but in these last days he has spoken to us by his Son."[61] Not the law, but the Lord Jesus is the culmination of God's message to mankind, and the pattern to which we are called. When Paul encourages believers toward Christian growth he does not put law before them as their aim or ultimate goal, but Christ: "Be imitators of me, *as I am of Christ.*"[62]

The Spirit-Law Antithesis

A recurrent theme in Paul's epistles is the power of the Holy Spirit in the life of the Christian, but the corollary to this is the apostle's insistence that the Spirit is doing his work apart from the law: "But now we are released from the law, having died to that which held us captive, so that we serve in the new way of the Spirit and not in the old way of the written code."[63] Here are statements about the believer's position. We are those who have died to the law, and it no longer holds us captive; we maintain no obligation to it, and it has no claim on us. It is important to again recognize that Paul is

60. Betz, *Galatians*, 179.

61. Heb 1:1.

62. 1 Cor 11:1 (emphasis added).

63. Rom 7:6.

saying nothing here about our obligation to holiness. Indeed, in the latter half of the verse, he takes it for granted that Christians do serve God, but they do so in a new way, without reference to the law, to the written code.

An important covenantal difference that enables New Testament obedience is the giving of the Holy Spirit. This, too, is a development of salvation history. The fact that the Holy Spirit, the third person of the Trinity, was active throughout the entire Old Testament is demonstrably true. He was there in the very beginning, hovering over the face of the waters at creation. He came upon men and women to empower and enable them. Samson, Gideon, and Saul were but a few of whom we read, "the Spirit of the Lord came upon him mightily."[64] But the old covenant experience of the Spirit did not have the fullness that the new covenant believer knows. Jesus affirmed that his death, resurrection, and ascension to heaven were necessary for the Spirit to come: "It is to your advantage that I go away, for if I do not go away, the Helper will not come to you. But if I go, I will send him to you."[65] Pentecost was the day the Holy Spirit arrived on the earth in this new way. Paul also tells the Ephesians that they "were sealed with the promised Holy Spirit, who is the guarantee of our inheritance."[66] This eschatological development accompanies the new creation that God works in those who believe in Jesus. It is something that old covenant saints did not know. To be clear, salvation has always been by faith. But the relationship Old Testament saints enjoyed with the Holy Spirit is not the same as the intimacy and nearness we now enjoy, and that prompts Paul to say we have the spirit of adoption.

The Spirit lives within believers, and empowers them to obedience and conformity to Christ. But is it the Spirit's work to enable law-keeping? Does conformity to Christ take this form? This is the position of some theologians: "Since Christ, the capital 'L' Law-keeper, is now being formed in us, and dwells—through the

64. Judg 14:6, NASB.

65. John 16:7.

66. Eph 1:13–14.

Spirit—in us, we are now lowercase 'l' law-keepers";[67] "With the gospel and in Christ, united to him by faith, the law is no longer my enemy but my friend. Why? Because *God* is no longer my enemy but my friend. And the law, *his* will, the law in its moral core, as reflective of his character and concerns eternally inherent in his own person and so of what pleases him, is now my friendly guide for life in fellowship with God."[68]

The New Testament, however, doesn't state that believers become law-keepers. Rather, they become fruit-bearers, something far different. As Paul stipulated in Romans 7:4, the believer now belongs to another, "to him who has been raised from the dead, in order that we may bear fruit for God."[69] Does the Spirit enable us to keep the law? If that is the case, Paul does not teach this. The apostle has spoken of the "old way of the written code" and the "new way of the Spirit." The new way is not simply a Spirit-enabled service in the old way. It is a contrast between them. The incongruity of these two ways is a consistent stance he takes whenever he instructs believers about their service to God. This, too, belongs to the unfolding of salvation history:

> Paul equates the incompatibility between the "flesh" and the "Spirit" with the incompatibility between the "Law" and the "Spirit." Paul places both the "flesh" and "Law" over against the Spirit not because the Law is inherently evil but because both "flesh" and "Law" belong to a previous sphere of existence, that is, a pre-Christian disposition associated with a previous phase of salvation-history.[70]

Insofar as we fail to recognize the law as properly part of the old covenant, we will fail to recognize the method God now uses to conform us to his Son.

While rule-of-life believers are always very clear that the law plays no part in our justification before God, they do not maintain

67. Green, *Covenant and Commandment*, 86.

68. Gaffin, *By Faith, Not by Sight*, 117–18.

69. Rom 7:1–4.

70. Bertone, *Law of the Spirit*, 139–40.

the contrast between the law and the Spirit when it comes to sanctification. Hoekema writes, "The Christian life, we conclude, must be a law-formed life. Though believers must not try to keep God's law as a means of earning their salvation, they are nevertheless enjoined to do their best to keep this law as a means of showing their thankfulness to God for the salvation they have received as a gift of grace. For believers, law-keeping is an expression of Christian love and the way to Christian freedom; it is equivalent to walking by the Spirit."[71]

The New Testament doesn't direct believers to keep God's law as a way of demonstrating their thankfulness to God, nor to do their best to keep God's law. It's impossible to fit a "do your best" attitude into anything Paul teaches about the law. It should likewise be clear that Paul does not present freedom as a result of keeping the law: "For freedom Christ has set us free; stand firm therefore, and do not submit again to a yoke of slavery."[72] Freedom we have, but it is freedom from the law. The apostle has ascribed slavery and its mastery over us to the law, in the hands of our sinful nature.[73] The dominion of sin comes from the obligation to keep the law and the condemnation that results when we fail to do so. Instead of law-keeping, our thankfulness takes the form of becoming a living-sacrifice (dying to self) as the spiritual service of worship we render to God.[74]

In Galatians 2, Paul speaks of building and tearing down—specifically, "if I rebuild what I tore down, I prove myself to be a transgressor."[75] Paul has "torn down" the law for any part of salvation in Christ. If we bring it back, it is plain that it represents a transgression against the righteousness of Christ wholly apart from law. Vincent Smiles comments, "The event of faith, when God's call was heard and accepted, and the Spirit was received (3:2–5), was also the event of the law's destruction. It ought to be evident, therefore,

71. Hoekema, "Reformed Perspective," 88.
72. Gal 5:1.
73. Rom 6:14.
74. Rom 12:1.
75. Gal 2:18.

that to 'rebuild' the law is to betray God's call in Christ, and it is that *betrayal of Christ* that comprises the 'transgression' of 2:18."[76] Burton agrees: "So far from being the case that I commit sin by violating the statutes of the law, it is, on the contrary, the fact that if I build up again those commands of the law which I broke down, I show myself therein a transgressor."[77] Does Paul only refer to justification? It is clear from the later chapters of Galatians that he also disavows the law as an instrument of sanctification. Longenecker has aptly summarized, "any return to the Law for either justification, or as in the case of the Galatians, for sanctification is a return to the 'weak and beggarly elements' and a renunciation of Christ."[78]

Paul's consternation with the Galatian Christians continues, and it is exactly the reintroduction of law that he decries: "Let me ask you only this: Did you receive the Spirit by works of the law or by hearing with faith? Are you so foolish? Having begun by the Spirit, are you now being perfected by the flesh?"[79] At the start, the apostle contrasts the works of law with the hearing of faith. How does one receive the Spirit of God? Quite plainly it is by faith, by belief in the person of the Lord Jesus. This is how one begins the Christian life. Once we have been born again and are made new creatures, how do we go on with God? Paul asks incredulously if the Galatians actually believe it is on a different basis from how they started. This is his clear meaning, with the question "are you now being perfected by the flesh?" Do you imagine you can grow in your Christian life by adherence to the law? Such is a fleshly undertaking, says Paul.

His questions resume as he asks, "Does he who supplies the Spirit to you and works miracles among you do so by works of the law, or by hearing with faith—just as Abraham 'believed God, and it was counted to him as righteousness'?"[80] Here, too, Paul asks about their Christian life: How do they live it? How do they sus-

---

76. Smiles, *Gospel and the Law*, 160 (emphasis his).

77. Burton, *Galatians*, 130.

78. Longenecker, *Paul, Apostle of Liberty*, 141.

79. Gal 3:2–3.

80. Gal 3:5–6.

tain it? He disavows any role for the law as an aid to their ongoing relationship with the risen Lord or for growth in Christ-likeness: "This question picks up the two different aspects of the Galatians' experience of the Spirit (the initial and the ongoing). What Paul is stressing is that neither the initial experience of the Spirit nor his ongoing activity among believers is dependent upon their doing the works of the law."[81]

Further on in this same chapter, he makes another surprisingly blunt statement: "Now it is evident that no one is justified before God by the law, for 'The righteous shall live by faith.' *But the law is not of faith*, rather 'The one who does them shall live by them.'"[82] Some have opined that what Paul protests against is that the Galatians are trying to keep the law apart from faith. If they would approach the law through faith, this would supply what they have been missing. But the apostle leaves no room for a faith-enabled law, or for the idea that, if the Galatians would simply bring their faith to bear on their adherence to law, all would be well.

Nor is it plausible that he is opposing a misunderstanding of the law. Rather, it is a declaration of contrast, not only between law and grace, but between law and faith. Westerholm comments, "To say that the Mosaic code is based on faith, not works, is blatantly incompatible with what Paul says elsewhere. In Philippians 3:6, 9 he contrasts the righteousness based on law (ἐν νόμῳ, ἐκ νόμου) [in law, of law] with that of faith; there is no hint that the former designations refer to a *distortion* of the law."[83]

It is vital to see that, in all of Paul's discussion of law, he presents an unfolding narrative of God's dealings with mankind that consigns the law to a prior age. Indeed, the law was the covenantal substance of God's relationship to Israel. But under the new covenant, the relationship to law has changed. We are in a new era, one where the Spirit's indwelling of believers means that we pattern ourselves not after the law, but after the risen Christ as the Sprit enables us.

81. Kruse, "Paul, the Law, and the Spirit," 112.
82. Gal 3:11–12 (emphasis added).
83. Westerholm, *Perspectives*, 326 (emphasis his).

4

Are Believers Obligated to the Law?

As it is impossible to be justified by the Law, it is equally impossible to be sanctified by the Law . . . he even puts it as strongly as this, that not only can a man not be sanctified by the Law, but it is actually true to say that the Law is a hindrance to sanctification, and that it aggravates the problem of sanctification . . . not only can a man not sanctify himself by observance of the Law; the Law is even a hindrance and an obstacle to sanctification.

—Martyn Lloyd-Jones[1]

MANY CHRISTIANS HAVE A somewhat ill-defined view of their relationship to the law, but Robert McQuilken summarizes a common perspective: "What was true of Moses is true of every believer today. By the grace of God he is enabled through supernatural power to keep the law of God—*but never perfectly.* Because he is not under law, he is therefore not under condemnation."[2] McQuilken's solution to the problem of law asserts that, with the coming of the Holy Spirit, this brings the Christian to a place where the Spirit empowers him or her to

1. Lloyd-Jones, *Romans*, 5.
2. McQuilken, *God's Law*, 47 (emphasis his).

keep the law, but only sometimes. Holiness takes the form of law-keeping, of conformity to the Decalogue, but has a built-in accommodation for the handicap of our sinful bent. (McQuilken, too, distinguishes between moral and ceremonial law, and thus discharges the believer from most of the Torah.) As I'll demonstrate with a few examples from Christian history, this position isn't unique, but it is problematic. Returning Christians to an obligation to the Decalogue paraphrases Paul to say, "I through the law died to the law for justification, so that I might be sanctified by keeping the law." This does not seem far from McQuilken's position, but it is far indeed from the apostle Paul's.

The Law in Protestant History

How did historical tradition come to see the law in this way, as applicable to regulate the lives of Christians? The principals of the Reformation viewed the law in the three traditional divisions and uses, in an attempt to make sense of it for today. There was common agreement on the three categories of moral, civil, and ceremonial, but some divergence on the uses of the law. Martin Luther himself stated only two uses for the law. The first use is to govern society and maintain order. The second is to reveal sin and to convict mankind of it. Luther called these two uses the political and the spiritual.[3] But later thinkers in the Lutheran tradition went beyond him to embrace a third use. The Lutheran *Book of Concord* outlines this as follows: "The Law of God is used (1) to maintain external discipline and respectability against dissolute, disobedient people and (2) to bring such people to a recognition of their sins. (3) It is also used when those who have been born anew through God's Spirit, converted to the Lord, and had the veil of Moses removed for them, live and walk in the law. A dispute arose among a few theologians concerning this third and final use of the Law."[4] One can detect in the first use a civil purpose; that is,

3. Althaus, *Theology of Martin Luther*, 254.
4. Kolb et al., *Book of Concord*, 587.

to maintain domestic and national order. That use is particular to a theocracy—which Israel was. Some in fact hold to this even today. Theonomy is the view that we should govern society by God's laws, even to regulate the conduct of unbelievers. Theonomy has few adherents in the mainstream of theological thought.

Alongside the *Book of Concord*, within Reformed theology the "third use of the law" is also traced to John Calvin. In the *Institutes of the Christian Religion*, Calvin presents an exposition of the significance of God's law, culminating in the third use:

> The third and principal use of the law, which pertains more closely to the proper use of the law, finds its place among believers in whose hearts the Spirit of God already lives and reigns.
>
> Again, because we need not only teaching but also exhortation, the servant of God will also avail himself of this benefit of the law: by frequent meditation upon it to be aroused to obedience, be strengthened in it, and be drawn back from the slippery path of transgression. In this way the saints must press on: for, however eagerly they may in accordance with the Spirit strive toward God's righteousness, the listless flesh always so burdens them that they do not proceed with due readiness. The law is to the flesh like a whip to an idle and balky ass, to arouse it to work. Even for a spiritual man not yet free of the weight of the flesh the law remains a constant sting that will not let him stand still.[5]

The *Westminster Confession of Faith*, the Puritan expression of Calvinism, repeats this view:

> 5. The moral law doth forever bind all, as well justified persons as others, to the obedience thereof; and that not only in regard of the matter contained in it, but also in respect of the authority of God the Creator who gave it. Neither doth Christ in the gospel any way dissolve, but much strengthen, this obligation.

5. Calvin, *Institutes*, 2.7.12.

6. It is likewise of use to the regenerate, to restrain their corruptions, in that it forbids sin, and the threatenings of it serve to show what even their sins deserve, and what afflictions in this life they may expect for them, although freed from the curse thereof threatened in the law. The promises of it, in like manner, show them God's approbation of obedience, and what blessings they may expect upon the performance thereof; although not as due to them by the law as a covenant of works: so as a man's doing good, and refraining from evil, because the law encourageth to the one, and deterreth from the other, is no evidence of his being under the law, and not under grace.[6]

Louis Berkhof, an influential theologian of the previous century, presents the law as "a rule of life for believers, reminding them of their duties and leading them in the way of life and salvation. This use of the law is denied by the antinomians."[7] Berkhof's statements are consistent with Calvin and the *Westminster Confession*, and with later confessional tradition represented by *Westminster*, but he does not support these claims in his *Manual of Christian Doctrine* by any biblical text. For something that plays so large a role in the life of the Christian, one would expect such claims to have biblical support.

The rule-of-life view (or third use) crosses some otherwise-wide chasms in various theological traditions. John Wesley, who would disagree with Calvin on predestination and election, nevertheless is one with him in this estimation of law. In his notes on Exodus, Wesley says,

When God was reconciled to them [Israel], he ordered the tables to be renewed, and wrote his law in them, which plainly intimates to us, that even under the gospel (of which the intercession of Moses was typical) the moral law should continue to oblige believers. Though Christ has redeemed us from the curse of the law, yet not

---

6. Westminster Assembly, *Confession of Faith*, 19:5–6.
7. Berkhof, *Manual of Christian Doctrine*, 308.

from the command of it, but still we are under the law to Christ.[8]

Wesley likewise held to a threefold use of the law, reserving the third for believers: "The third use of the law is, to keep us alive. It is the grand means whereby the blessed Spirit prepares the believer for larger communications of the life of God."[9]

Consistent with Calvin and Wesley, others (such as Cranfield) have sought to explain Paul by separating commandment from condemnation, and insisting it is only the latter we are free from: "The life promised for the man who is righteous by faith is, in the third place, described as a life characterized by freedom from the law, that is, from the law in the limited sense of the-law-as-condemning, or the law's condemnation (cf. 8:1)."[10] Cranfield is reading into Paul's statements something that is not there. Paul assigns the law's ability to kill to the commandment, not to a fear of condemnation:

> But sin, seizing an opportunity through the commandment, produced in me all kinds of covetousness. For apart from the law, sin lies dead. I was once alive apart from the law, but when the commandment came, sin came alive and I died. The very commandment that promised life proved to be death to me. For sin, seizing an opportunity through the commandment, deceived me and through it killed me. So the law is holy, and the commandment is holy and righteous and good.[11]

Cranfield further comments, "Paul has told the Roman Christians in 6.14 that they are 'not under the law, but under grace,' in order to encourage them to obey the imperatives of 6.12–13. Now in 7.1–6 he elucidates the statement, showing how it is true, how it has come about that they are free from the law's condemnation."[12]

---

8. Wesley, *Explanatory Notes*, 321.

9. Wesley, *Use of The Law*, 14.

10. Cranfield, *Romans*, 330.

11. Rom 7:8–12.

12. Cranfield, *Romans*, 331.

These claims call for an examination of what scripture presents. Does the New Testament teach the third use of the law? Is the law God's instrument for sanctifying the Christian?

These Christian thinkers cover the ground of how the Protestant tradition has dealt with the Ten Commandments. In their view, the moral law remains our standard, but it is a divided standard. We are obligated to obey the Ten Commandments, but there is no condemnation for any transgression of the law. This is common in the rule-of-life position, but it comes with problems. If the believer is free from condemnation, but not obligation to the law, it represents an essential redefinition of what the law is, of its very nature. It is no longer the Ten Commandments, but the Ten Suggestions. For if an obligation remains, yet there is no consequence, the very idea of a lawbreaker is moot.

Such a concept of dividing consequence from commandment is foreign to Paul's thinking, and introduces a change to the essence of the law, to its DNA. Seifrid recognizes this when he affirms, "When Paul speaks of 'the law' he has in view the commands given at Sinai, which cannot be detached from their authority to condemn without ceasing to be 'law.'"[13] It is worth emphasizing this point, because it is a central tenet of the claim that believers retain an obligation to the Decalogue, but are free from condemnation. Yet nothing in Paul's thought supports this division. It is consistent with his view of law as a unit that he likewise sees the law as consisting of both command and condemnation for the lawbreaker. We cannot sever these aspects of the law from one another without altering the definition of law, as given by God. To insist on obligation to law, yet without consequence for law-breaking, does not uphold the law.

What of the more common divisions and uses that Calvin, Westminster, and Berkhof present? The "third use" in one sense stands or falls on the validity of these distinctions, but Paul never makes such qualifications in his statements about law. Calvin groups the civil and ceremonial laws together, calling them "what

13. Seifrid, *Christ, Our Righteousness*, 126.

is proper to the ministry of Moses."[14] He seeks to dismiss this part of the law and claim an abiding obligation for the Decalogue, lifting it from its native soil of the Mosaic covenant. But as Paul shows in 2 Corinthians 3, the tablets of stone as an obligatory standard come to an end, along with the Mosaic covenant itself coming to an end. It was not the civil or ceremonial laws inscribed on the tablets, but the "Ten Words" given at Sinai.

Paul is careful with his words. He does not assign evil to the law. On the contrary, he affirms it is holy, righteous, and good. He marks the culprit to be our indwelling sin which—when combined with law—produces death. It is a kind of toxic combination within us. The illustration is imperfect, because there is no time when sin is not lethal all by itself, but as the combination of ammonia and bleach produces toxic fumes, our sinful nature—when combined with the law—both reveals and increases sin. Jason Meyer refers to this as "the disastrous duo of the flesh and the law.[15] The law may be good, but we are not. The law is diagnostic, showing sin, but it is never therapeutic; it cannot heal nor even provide help in overcoming sin.

This is why giving the role to law that the "third use" does is problematic. Can the law function in our lives such that "the servant of God will also avail himself of this benefit of the law: by frequent meditation upon it to be aroused to obedience"?[16] Note that it is not only a record of God's faithfulness to Israel, a covenant between God and the children of Jacob, but the "third use" ascribes more to the law than these things. The "third use" assigns to the commandments the ability to bring forth obedience. From the biblical evidence, we must conclude that this is an unlawful use of the law. Paul never assigns such a function to the law in the believer's life—not even to the Ten Commandments. Recall what the apostle has said about the law. In addition to revealing sin, Paul is so bold as to say that the law also arouses sin.[17] He calls the law

14. Calvin, *Romans*, 45.
15. Meyer, *End of the Law*, 47.
16. Calvin, *Institutes*, 2.7.12.
17. Rom 7:5.

the power of sin,[18] a ministry of death and condemnation.[19] He says the law is not of faith.[20] He addresses believers when he writes these things, and he draws these examples from the Decalogue when he speaks of law.

Calvin cites no Scripture to support such a use of the law in the believer's life. Indeed, his view is not based on exposition, but instead on his conviction of God's unity of purpose through all ages. Even if he did not express it in the same terms as later covenant theologians would, this idea is certainly present in Calvin's thinking. As Westerholm puts it, "Calvin insists, the law cannot conflict with the gospel, since both have the same divine source."[21] But such a view rests on a definition of conflict that was not in the mind of the apostle. To say that the law cannot justify, cannot sanctify, while the gospel can do both, is not to imply conflicting purposes in the mind of God. Rather, it is to recognize that God gave the law for different reasons. To acknowledge these differences is to embrace his purposes in salvation history, which we examined in the previous chapter.

Upholding the Law

One verse used to defend the idea that believers should now seek to live by the law is the final verse of Romans 3. Paul anticipates the accusation of his opponents, and asks, "Do we then overthrow the law by this faith? By no means! On the contrary, we uphold the law."[22] Is Paul referring to the law as commandment here, to the Decalogue? Does he mean to say that faith exercised rightly will lead Christians back to the law? Many believe this is the sense of Paul's protest. Far from leading to license and careless living, his doctrine does the opposite: "We uphold the law." While it is

18. 1 Cor 15:56.
19. 2 Cor 3:7, 8.
20. Gal 3:12.
21. Westerholm, *Perspectives*, 95.
22. Rom 3:31.

true that faith leads to obedience, this is not Paul's point here. The context of the passage offers a different view. Paul has finished an indictment of both Jew and gentile as under the judgment of God. He has stated that the righteousness of God has been manifested apart from the law, although the Law and the Prophets bear witness to it.[23]

Readers may have asked what Paul has done with the witness of the patriarchs and the history of God's dealings with the nation of Israel. Are these of no value now that righteousness through faith has come? It is this question Paul means to answer, and he does so with a resounding affirmation of the patriarchs and the entire Old Testament history. Verse 21 shows this, in a way (at least through editorial decisions in the English Standard Version.) In the first half of the verse, "law" is in lowercase. This denotes the use of the word as synonymous with commandment, and adherence to statutes. Paul has said that God imputes to us his righteousness apart from such law-keeping. But the second half has the word "Law" in uppercase, and with the additional phrase "and the Prophets."

This use of the word corresponds to "Law" as Torah, as Scripture. In short, verses 21 and 31 are in full agreement, showing that the Old Testament contained justification by faith, and is no novelty with Paul. Stifler comments, "Paul will teach nothing contradictory to what he has already [in Romans] called the Holy Scriptures (1:2) For the word 'law' here [in v. 31] does not mean the ceremonial or even the moral law, but the whole Old Testament. 'We establish the law.' The next chapter shows how."[24] Greek scholar Henry Alford concurs:

> Many commentators have taken this verse (being misled in some cases by its place at the end of the chapter) as standing by itself, and have gone into the abstract grounds why faith does not make void the law (or moral obedience); which, however true, *have no place here*: the design being to show that the law contained this very

23. Rom 3:21.
24. Stifler, *Romans*, 70.

doctrine, and was founded in the promise to Abraham on a covenant embracing Jews and Gentiles.[25]

Ragnar Bring writes, "It is therefore perfectly logical for Paul to refer to the Old Testament for illustrations and proofs of what he proclaims."[26] A. Andrew Das likewise comments, "Romans 4 neatly supports Paul's argument in 3:27–31: the Mosaic law, understood in the sense of Torah/Scripture, had pointed to salvation by faith all along."[27]

The fourth chapter of Romans flows seamlessly from Paul's statement of upholding the law, and is his presentation of evidence. He cites the examples of Abraham and David, intending to show that the very same Scriptures that the Jewish nation trusts in proclaim justification by faith, righteousness apart from works. No, says Paul, I am not in any way overthrowing the law, I am in fact showing how entirely consistent my doctrine is with what one reads in the Old Testament. Paul is saying nothing here about faith and the Decalogue. Lifted from its context, the end of Romans 3 has led many to conclude that Paul is, in essence, saying that we who are Christians are led back to the law, to practice it and keep the Ten Commandments. But we cannot harmonize that with what Paul will say a few chapters on, and also in the Galatian epistle. The emphasis on chapter 4 has nothing to do with confronting supposed antinomianism, but rather to prove that justification by faith apart from works is replete throughout the entire Old Testament.

Others doubt that Paul refers to the Old Testament at the end of Romans 3. Moo argues, "When denoting that function [as Scripture] of the OT, he uses 'the law and the Prophets' (v. 21) or the 'Scripture' (Gal. 3:8). Nowhere does he use 'law' by itself to indicate this witnessing role of the OT."[28] But Paul does in fact do this in Galatians: "Tell me, you who desire to be under the law, do you not

---

25. Alford, *Greek Testament*, 350.

26. Bring, *Galatians*, 16.

27. Das, *Paul, the Law*, 199.

28. Moo, *Romans*, 254.

listen to the law?"[29] He then goes on to give the story of Sarah and Hagar, and to interpret the allegory for the Galatians. Here Paul uses the word "law" apart from a reference to "the Prophets," and he clearly uses the term to refer to the biblical record of the Old Testament. When summarizing his argument in Galatians 3:21, he even exchanges the word "law" for "Scripture": "But what does the Scripture say? 'Cast out the slave woman and her son, for the son of the slave woman shall not inherit with the son of the free woman.'"[30]

Notwithstanding Moo's doubts on the word "law" here in a witnessing role, he is not arguing for the third use of the law.

> The stress on *faith* as establishing the law suggest that it is law as fulfilled in and through our faith in Christ that Paul thinks of here. In 8:4, Paul will argue that those who are in Christ and who "walk according to the Spirit" have the law fulfilled "in them," in the sense that their relationship to Christ by faith fully meets the demands of God's law.[31]

Moo touches on a theme that I will later expand upon: the important difference between keeping the law and fulfilling it. What is the righteous requirement of the law, but holiness? "You shall be holy to me, for I the Lord am holy and have separated you from the peoples, that you should be mine."[32] God separated the nation of Israel, marked it out from the surrounding nations, and because of their covenant relationship with God they were to be holy. They failed in this, as their subsequent history demonstrates.

The New Testament believer fulfills holiness, the righteous requirement of the law, by paradoxically not pursuing the law. Paul says we walk not according to flesh, but according to the Spirit. He has told the Galatians that if they are led by the Spirit, they are not under the law,[33] and also that the law is not of faith.[34] The Spirit

29. Gal 4:21.
30. Gal 4:30.
31. Moo, *Romans*, 255.
32. Lev 20:26.
33. Gal 5:18.
34. Gal 3:12.

does not direct us to the law as the substance of our Christian life, but to the Lord Jesus. On the path of conformity to Christ, the law (and its righteous requirement of holiness) will be fulfilled. But the opposite is not true. If we focus on keeping the law, this will not lead to conformity to Christ. This distinction is vital to understand, and it is a fundamental difference with the rule-of-life view. Paul never presents the law, as Wesley asserts, to keep us alive; nor, as Berkhof claims, to lead us in the way of life and salvation. Rather, he presents the law as what kills us and enslaves us. Christians enjoy freedom, but the death of Christ, a law-fulfilling death, is what brings that freedom.

Calvin says that one of the benefits of the law is that the believer will "be aroused to obedience, be strengthened in it, and be drawn back from the slippery path of transgression." But the apostle Paul states the opposite. Rather than aroused to obedience, he was instead aroused to sin: "If it had not been for the law, I would not have known sin. For I would not have known what it is to covet if the law had not said, 'You shall not covet.' But sin, seizing an opportunity through the commandment, produced in me all kinds of covetousness. For apart from the law, sin lies dead. I was once alive apart from the law, but when the commandment came, sin came alive and I died" (Rom 7:7–9). He calls the Law "the power of sin" in 1 Corinthians 15:56. Again, it is not a ceremonial or a civil part of the law that Paul says was, as it were, the murder weapon, but it was the "moral law"—the tenth commandment—that sin used to slay him.

Another proof frequently cited that the law continues as a means of sanctification is what Jesus says in the Sermon on the Mount. A. W. Pink writes, "So far from the Law being abolished by the coming of Christ into this world, He Himself emphatically stated, 'Think not that I came to destroy the Law and the Prophets (the enforcers thereof): I am come not to destroy, but to fulfill. For verily I say unto you, Till heaven and earth pass, one jot or one tittle shall in nowise pass from the law, till all be fulfilled' (Matt 5:17, 18). True, the Christian is not under the Law as a Covenant of Works or as a ministration of condemnation, but he *is* under it as a rule of life and a means of sanctification."[35]

Pink believes that the law's demands have a continuing claim upon the life of the Christian, but think through the implications of this. No Christian may eat pork, or catfish, for these transgress the dietary restrictions found in the law. Any Christian who plants an apple tree in his backyard must not eat any fruit from it for four years. Many people would doubtless relegate these laws to civil or ceremonial categories (and so insist that they are no longer binding), but one would also have to admit that these represent jots and tittles of the law which they are abrogating—the very thing that according to Matthew 5 must not be done. In other words, such a view is inconsistent with its own claim about the law. Any assertion that the law is our rule of life by necessity comes with this parsing of it. Pink has an assumption of the moral, civil, and ceremonial division of the law, but in light of the breadth of Jesus' statement in Matthew 5, it is a fair question to ask whether the view that only the moral law continues in force is itself undermining Jesus' words in this chapter.

Moreover, by arguing as he does, Pink presses for more continuity than is defensible from the rest of the New Testament witness to the law. David. E. Holwerda, though standing in the rule-of-life tradition, offers a counterweight to this:

> Even though Jesus affirms the ongoing validity of the law until the close of the age, the Christian has no direct access to that validity apart from the fulfillment in Christ. The fact that something is required by a specific Old Testament commandment does not directly dictate the shape of Christian obedience. Only as fulfilled and radicalized in the teaching and life of Jesus does the Old Testament law retain its validity until the close of the age.[36]

When he does refer to the law, Jesus demonstrates the principle I have been arguing for. That is, the law is not inconsistent

---

35. Pink, *Ten Commandments*, 9.
36. Holwerda, *Jesus and Israel*, 132–33.

with God's will, but not coextensive with it. The repeated contrasts drawn by Jesus in the Sermon on the Mount show this: "You have heard that it was said to those of old, 'You shall not murder; and whoever murders will be liable to judgment.' But I say to you that everyone who is angry with his brother will be liable to judgment."[37] Several more such comparisons follow, all of the same formula. Jesus quotes a portion of the law (including the Decalogue), then raises the standard higher than what the law pronounced. And the authority of Jesus himself is the basis for these statements, rather than any rabbinical tradition. This, too, is another reason why the Christian does not look to the Decalogue as the ultimate measure of how to please God, or of his eternal will. Rather, we look to his beloved Son, the one in whom he is well pleased, and who always demonstrated God's love and holiness—especially when those demonstrations far exceed the law.

The law does indeed remain binding until fulfilled, as Jesus stated in Matthew 5. But does the law remain unfulfilled until the present time? In his post-resurrection appearance to the two men on the Emmaus Road, we find Jesus answering this question: "And beginning with Moses and all the Prophets, he interpreted to them in all the Scriptures the things concerning himself."[38] Certainly all that was prophesied of Jesus from the manner of his birth, his miracles, the scattering of the Twelve, and a host of other incidents are all fulfillment of prophecy, and fulfillment of types and shadows. But there is a way in which Jesus fulfills the law that encompasses finality and completion, and that is by his death. In Galatians 3, Paul says, "Christ redeemed us from the curse of the law by becoming a curse for us—for it is written, 'Cursed is everyone who is hanged on a tree.'"[39] Paul is referencing Deuteronomy 21:23. The preceding verse is important as well: "And if a man has committed a crime punishable by death and he is put to death, and you hang him on a tree, his body shall not remain all night on the tree, but you shall

---

37. Matt 5:22–23.
38. Luke 24:27.
39. Gal 3:13.

bury him the same day, for a hanged man is cursed by God."[40] There is a twofold way in which the Lord Jesus fulfills this. Though he had no sin of his own, yet he took the place of the sinner, as one who had committed a crime punishable by death. And in his death on the cross Jesus fulfills the law, and exhausts its curses and claims. Law has no claim on one who has met its demands. His death reckoned as our death discharges us from the law.

Christ, the End of the Law

The tenth chapter of Romans is part of a discussion by the apostle about the nation of Israel in God's prophetic plan, her restoration and future. In the midst of this, he writes: "For, being ignorant of the righteousness of God, and seeking to establish their own, they did not submit to God's righteousness. For Christ is the end of the law for righteousness to everyone who believes."[41] There has been much disagreement about what Paul means by the statement of Christ as "the end of the law," and it is due to the meaning of one word. Indeed, Thomas Schreiner terms this "the never-ending debate that rages on this verse."[42] The Greek word τέλος is translated as "end," but it can also mean "goal" or "aim." For example, in 1 Timothy, Paul writes, "The aim [τέλος] of our charge is love that issues from a pure heart and a good conscience and a sincere faith."[43] The question is whether Paul is saying that, with Christ, our relationship to law has ended, or whether the law remains as something that points to Christ, and continues to direct believers to Christ as its ultimate goal. But is viewing the question as a sharp dichotomy the best approach?

The laws outlining the sacrifices are an especially rich trove of Christ as the goal. The Levitical offerings, for example, all point to the work of Jesus on our behalf, and are pleasing to his father.

---

40. Deut 21:22–23.

41. Rom 10:3–4.

42. Schreiner, *Law and Its Fulfillment*, 134.

43. 1 Tim 1:5.

He gave himself up wholly and completely to the Father's will, as typified in the burnt offering. "He is our peace,"[44] thus the peace offering points to him. "For our sake he made him to be sin who knew no sin, so that in him we might become the righteousness of God."[45] The sin offering exemplifies his sacrifice for us. When we come to Aaron the high priest, the New Testament identifies the office as pointing to Jesus: "We have such a high priest, one who is seated at the right hand of the throne of the Majesty in heaven, a minister in the holy places, in the true tent that the Lord set up, not man."[46] Many other parallels and illustrations could be cited to demonstrate that the Old Testament, including the law, pointed to Christ. Truly, he is the goal to which the law points.

But he is also the one who fulfills all these types and symbols, and in this sense he is the end of the law for righteousness. Because of this, it is doubtless the reason Paul makes statements of such finality with regard to the believer's current relationship to the law: "Through the law I died to the law," he tells the Galatians. The law says that everyone who hangs on a tree is cursed, and the Lord Jesus hung on Calvary's tree, absorbing its curse. Those who put their faith in Jesus are likewise reckoned to have died with him. In this way, through the law we died to the law (by Christ taking its full penalty). It has no more curse or condemnation for believers, and thus no more obligation.

While the Levitical sacrifices give us types of his death on our behalf, we cannot say that Jesus points us back to the Decalogue as a standard of righteousness, a rule of life. He himself far exceeded the law; in love, in devotion, in every way. If I am but pointed back to the Decalogue, I am turned to a lower standard than what the Lord Jesus calls his followers to: "You have heard it said . . . but I tell you." That the Decalogue points us to Christ is a less obvious case to make than the offerings. The Levitical sacrifices contained types in their very acts and actors. The Decalogue does not, save for the Sabbath being a type of our rest in Christ. Kaiser is correct

44. Eph 2:14.
45. 2 Cor 5:21.
46. Heb 8:1–2.

when he writes, "The law cannot be properly understood unless it moves toward the grand goal of pointing the believer toward the Messiah, Christ. The law remains God's law, not Moses' law (Rom 7:22, 8:7). It still is holy, just, good, and spiritual (Rom 7:12, 14) for the Israelite as well as for the believing Gentile."[47]

Kaiser's argument fits into viewing the law as God's wisdom, in keeping with what Brian Rosner described, rather than law as commandment. The law points us to Christ, but not back to itself. That is, having seen the goal as being the Lord Jesus, we do not reach the goal by returning to what pointed to it. Arguing for the law as an aid in promoting holiness clashes with what Paul has earlier said in Romans, that the law does not promote holiness, but instead promotes sin. It is important to revisit this point and to again make clear what the apostle says. Yes, the law is holy and righteous and good, but our Adamic nature is anything but. The law, in combination with our old self, increases sin. The law is not an obligation for those in Christ, because we have a different head and a different position. No longer in Adam, and no longer earthly, we are in Christ and seated with him in the heavenlies.

Barrett's translation of Romans 10:4 brings a helpful perspective on how it is that Christ is both end and goal of the law:

> For Christ, by realizing righteousness for every believer, proves to be the end of the law . . . The word τέλος means not only 'termination' but also 'purpose,' or 'intention,' and the key to the present passage is to be found in the words 'by realizing righteousness' (literally 'unto righteousness'—'unto' expressing purpose or goal). Christ is the end of the law, with a view not to anarchy but to righteousness. He puts an end to the law, not by destroying all that the law stood for, but by realizing it.[48]

The primary truth Paul has in mind here is the establishment of righteousness, and on what basis is it? He describes two types: by law, or by faith. The only way we can stand before God is through the righteousness of faith. To choose righteousness by

47. Kaiser, "Law as God's Guidance," 188.

48. Barrett, *Romans*, 197.

law is to set aside both God's divinely appointed path and the work of Christ. While the rule-of-life view affirms this faith, it goes on to state that, although law forms no basis for justification, it does form a basis for sanctification. May we conclude that, due to our changed position as "in Christ" and the Spirit's guidance, he enables our keeping of the law? Paul has repeatedly contrasted the Spirit and the law, and conjoined sin and the law in such a way that makes this path both dubious and unnecessary. We fulfill the law and its righteous requirement of holiness, but we do not do so by striving to keep the law. We instead become imitators of God and of Christ, fruit-bearers whose ability to bring forth fruit comes from our death to the law.

Using the Law Lawfully

At the start of 1 Timothy, where Paul writes, "we know that the law is good if one uses it lawfully,"[49] he says several important things. Echoing his sentiment of Romans 7:12—that the law is holy, righteous, and good—he affirms the law's provenance with God. Paul has never ascribed evil to the law. Even as the promise to Abraham came from God, so also the law was of God. But he also affirms that there is a lawful use of it. Is Paul referring to the three uses of the law we earlier considered? "These came to be called the *usus politicus* (to restrain evil), the *usus pedagogus* (to lead to Christ) and the *usus normativus* (to determine the conduct of believers)."[50] Recalling that Paul has said that through the law comes the knowledge of sin (the *usus pedagogus*), these verses can only fit into this category, but the commentators who support the rule-of-life view have taken a different approach.

Using the law lawfully is a pun Paul employs make his point, that the opponents he mentions in 1:7 do not understand the basics of the topic. They want to be teachers of the law, but they are incorrect about the right application of it. When Paul goes on to

49. 1 Tim 1:8.
50. Stott, *Guard the Truth*, 47.

say that "the law is not laid down for the just," the question arises, whom is he describing? The word "just" is *dikaio,* a term that is synonymous with righteousness and justification. It is the word Paul uses so often in Romans to describe our standing before God. He is not ashamed of the gospel because in it the righteousness of God is revealed.[51] Believers are justified freely by God's grace.[52] In Acts 13, Paul preaches in Antioch and says to his audience, "and by Him everyone who believes is justified from all things from which you could not be justified by the law of Moses."[53] All of these references are the same root word.

But not all think that Paul is describing Christians when he says "the just." Stott says this

> cannot refer to those who are righteous in the sense of "justified," since Paul insists elsewhere that the justified still do need the law for their sanctification. Nor can it be taken to mean that some people exist who are so righteous that they do not need the law to guide them, but only that some people think they are. Similarly, when Jesus said, "I have not come to call the righteous but sinners to repentance," he did not mean that there are some righteous people who do not need to be called to repentance, but only that some think they are. In a word, "the righteous" in these contexts means "the self-righteous."[54]

Paul has addressed such persons in the early chapters of Romans, applying the law specifically to those who imagined themselves to be righteous. Throughout Romans 2 and 3, Paul has methodically

---

51. Rom 1:17.

52. Rom 3:24.

53. Acts 13:39, NKJV (emphasis added).

54. Stott, *Guard the Truth,* 48. As evidence that the justified still need the law for their sanctification, Stott cites two verses from Romans 8:4, where Paul says, "in order that the righteous requirement of the law might be fulfilled in us, who walk not according to the flesh but according to the Spirit," and 13:8, "the one who loves another has fulfilled the law." In neither of these passages is the law set forth as a standard or a guide to which believers refer. Both passages use the word "fulfill" (not "keep," "obey," or "adhere to"), and Paul has always made a distinction between keeping and fulfilling the law.

shown that the idea of human righteousness is fiction. Apart from Christ, none is righteous, no not one: "All have turned aside; together they have become worthless; no one does good, not even one." Paul has stated that the law is a means of revealing sin. Were we to grant, with Stott, that Paul's reference to "the righteous" is to the self-righteous who are deluded about their true condition, does the apostle find no application of the law to such people? This would make Paul to say that the law is of no use in revealing sin. If any needs to understand their own sin, it is the self-righteous.

Calvin has a slightly different perspective on Paul's meaning: "My answer is that Paul here calls righteous not those who are absolutely perfect—since no such men will be found—but those who aim at what is good as the chief desire of their hearts, so that their godly desire is like a voluntary law that needs no external pressure or restraint."[55] Such a position is at odds, however, with the third use of the law. Calvin has elsewhere characterized the law as a whip, and said, "even for a spiritual man not yet free of the weight of the flesh the law remains a constant sting that will not let him stand still."[56] A whip and a sting surely fit into the category of external pressure!

Contra Stott and Calvin, Henry Alford says that the just "therefore can only mean, righteous in the *Christian sense,* viz. by *justifying faith and sanctification of the Spirit* . . . one who is included in the actual righteousness of Christ by having put Him on, and so not *forensically amenable to the law*—partaker of the inherent righteousness of Christ, inwrought by the Spirit, which unites him to Him, and so not *morally needing it.*"[57] Along with Alford, Philip H. Towner says, "Paul asserts that it [the law] was not for Christians ('the righteous') but for unbelievers. In this context, 'the righteous' . . . are Christian believers who through their genuine conversion produce the self-giving love (1:5) that fulfills the law."[58]

---

55. Calvin, *Second Epistle*, 193.

56. Calvin, *Institutes*, 2.7.12.

57. Alford, *Greek Testament*, 306 (emphasis his).

58. Towner, *Letters to Timothy and Titus*, 124.

E. K. Simpson concurs: "Not the saints as such, but the sinner, is the Law's target."[59]

Some raise the objection, as Calvin notes, "the apostle did not intend to argue about the whole office of the law, but views it in reference to men." In other words, it was not Paul's purpose to speak of all three uses of the law, but only to show its place in pointing out the evil of man's heart and deeds. Following this line of reasoning, one should not look for a repudiation of the third use of the law here in 1 Timothy. Yet no commentator claims that Paul is setting the law before believers as a rule, only that he doesn't address it. Paul's consistent treatment of the law elsewhere, however, argues that he does here reject the third use. He warns believers against taking up the law for their Christian walk, speaks of it as the strength of sin, and says that believers are not under it. To continue in the same line of thought, that the law is not for believers, would be in agreement with what he writes in these other epistles. As Fee notes, "By saying the Law was not intended for 'the righteous,' Paul reflects a point made earlier in Galatians, that those who have the Spirit and bear its fruit have entered a sphere of existence in which the Law no longer performs its legal functions (Gal 5:22–23)."[60] Witherington agrees: "This entire discussion is much like what we find in Galatians 5–6, and we may note especially Gal 5:22–23, where Paul says that those who walk by the Spirit have gone beyond the realm of the law in a positive direction and thus do not need its correction."[61] Paul's doctrine is wonderfully consistent. Those who walk by the Spirit are not under the law, nor subject to its demands, because their Spirit-guided obedience has a higher standard than the Ten Commandments. The believer walking in love and imitating Christ does not have to concern himself with any other standard.

---

59. Simpson, *Pastoral Epistles*, 31.

60. Fee, *1 and 2 Timothy, Titus*, 10.

61. Witherington, *Letters and Homilies*, 195–96.

5

The Ten Commandments in the New Testament

We teach that the law had a beginning partly in order to show that the law had an ending; that it is not binding upon the Christian. Does that mean that the opposite of law is lawlessness? Certainly not! For the Christian, the opposite of law is not lawlessness but holy living under grace.

—Donald Grey Barnhouse[1]

Fulfilling the Law

IN CONSIDERING THE CHRISTIAN'S relationship to the Mosaic law, I have discussed how, while most theologians concede that the civil and ceremonial aspects of the law are no longer binding on believers, many still maintain a separate status for the Ten Commandments. I have demonstrated, however, that the New Testament reserves no special status for the Decalogue, but reveals that it, just like the rest of the law, is no longer binding on today's believers. Other theologians—even without reference to any explicit divisions of moral, civil, and ceremonial law—argue for an implicit obligation to the Ten Commandments for Christians

1. Barnhouse, *Romans*, 115.

based upon the fact that at several points the epistles seem to enjoin obedience to them. Paul tells the Romans,

> Owe no one anything, except to love each other, for the one who loves another has fulfilled the law. For the commandments, 'You shall not commit adultery, You shall not murder, You shall not steal, You shall not covet,' and any other commandment, are summed up in this word: 'You shall love your neighbor as yourself.' Love does no wrong to a neighbor; therefore love is the fulfilling of the law.[2]

He references commandments six, seven, eight, and ten positively, but is Paul putting these forth as the standard for the believer to follow? No, he is instead using them as a fulcrum for his argument for a superior standard, by no means inconsistent with what the Law commands, but exceeding it. This important distinction is sometimes obscured by rule-of-life believers. Anthony Hoekema, commenting on the Romans 13 passage, writes, "Paul here not only instructs believers to continue to fulfill the law; he also implies that, contrary to the opinion of some, there is no conflict between lawkeeping and love."[3] There is surely no conflict between law-keeping and love, but two important aspects are missing from Hoekema's description. First, nowhere does Paul tell believers, "Keep these commandments"; second, he *does* tell them that love is the standard they should pursue, and in so doing, the law will be fulfilled. But the opposite is not true. Paul does not say that in keeping the law, we will walk in love.

The distinction between keeping and fulfilling the law may seem at first to be an artificial one, but the statements the apostle makes about our relationship to the law support it. Hans Dieter Betz shows that Paul does this by "carefully distinguishing between the 'doing' and the 'fulfilling' of the Torah—the 'doing' of the Jewish Torah is not required for Christians, but the 'fulfilling' is."[4] Since Paul quotes the tenth commandment here in chapter

2. Rom 13:8–10.
3. Hoekema, "Reformed Perspective," 88.
4. Betz, *Galatians*, 275.

13 of Romans, is he simply being inconsistent with what he earlier said in chapter 7? It was the same commandment that Paul used as his example of what killed him, what aroused sin within him, and that he found impossible to keep. And he summarized his experience with the tenth commandment in 7:6 to say, "But now we are released from the law." If we are bound to both keep the law, but at the same time released from it, these two cannot coexist. Distinguishing between fulfilling and keeping solves the difficulty of how to treat the law that putting believers under obligation to it does not.

Paul also quotes the fifth commandment to the Ephesian church: "'Honor your father and mother' (this is the first commandment with a promise), 'that it may go well with you and that you may live long in the land.'" It is important to note that this citation comes after his interpretation of it. The apostolic command is, "Children, obey your parents in the Lord, for this is right" (Eph 6:1). In other words, Paul does not begin with the Mosaic commandment, but rather with his own apostolic instruction to the church. He quotes the fifth commandment to demonstrate that his own application is consistent with what the Decalogue requires, but goes beyond it. The idea of "honoring" in the Old Testament was very much tied to financial support, as is clear from Jesus' criticism of the Pharisaical twisting of the command:

> For Moses said, "Honor your father and your mother"; and, "Whoever reviles father or mother must surely die." But you say, "If a man tells his father or his mother, 'Whatever you would have gained from me is Corban'" (that is, given to God)—then you no longer permit him to do anything for his father or mother. (Mark 7:10–12)

The Pharisees had invented a kind of annuity that let them shelter money from the obligation to help their parents, and it is thus clear that honoring has to do with materially providing for someone. But Paul's interest goes beyond fulfilling a financial obligation. He is interested in the relationship, the spiritual component to the parent-child bond, which is why he extrapolates from the commandment to go beyond it, to loving obedience. This is another example of the apostolic use of the Decalogue in a fashion that exceeds the original.

In the many opportunities Paul had to appeal to the Ten Commandments when addressing problems in the churches, or in setting out a pattern for pleasing God, it is remarkable how infrequently he does so. In dealing with the Corinthians, a congregation with serious moral issues, the apostle repeats back to them a phrase that may have had currency in that city, "All things are lawful."[5] Somewhat surprisingly, Paul does not contradict this to say, "No, all things are not lawful." Rather, he answers with an implicit agreement, although he counters the statement with qualifiers of his own. "I will not be enslaved by anything," he says, and goes on to teach them about their identity as members of Christ. It is inconsistent to treat their bodies as belonging to anyone other than God: "You were bought with a price. So glorify God in your body."[6] Notably, in 1 Corinthians 6, Paul makes no appeal to the law to admonish these believers against immorality. The Hebrew Scriptures and Judaism unquestionably formed Paul's ethics, but he nevertheless does not quote commandments back to the Corinthians.[7] His own instruction, and their identity as joined to the risen Lord Jesus, their redemption—these are the ground of his teaching. Later on in 1 Corinthians 10, we again find the phrase "All things are lawful," and similarly, Paul directs them to what is better. Not all things are helpful, and not all things build up.[8] This time, the context is meat offered to idols. We have liberty, he says. We can eat whatever we want, but take care for your brothers and sisters whom you may offend. Concern for other believers, humil-

---

5. 1 Cor 6:12.

6. 1 Cor 6:20.

7. Cf. Rosner, *Paul, Scripture, and Ethics*, for an examination of how the apostle's ethics were formed by the Jewish Scriptures. Even though a basis of Paul's ethics is unquestionably the Old Testament Scriptures, his encounter with the risen Christ altered his guidance to his congregations to direct them to distinctively Christian (apostolic) commands, while in no way contradicting the Old Testament. Rosner's later work in *Paul and the Law: Keeping the Commandments of God* reflects this.

8. 1 Cor 10:23.

ity, and building others up are Paul's guiding principles here. One can argue these are not at odds with the law, and indeed they are not, but there are many places where the law does not go as far as apostolic instruction, nor is as nuanced as Paul's advice to his congregations.

Jason Meyer has provided a helpful summary on this point:

> This recognition that Christian behavior will "fulfill" the law even though the Christian believer is not under the law requires a different starting point for the discussion. I propose that one should begin with Christ and not with the individual Mosaic commands. The coming of Christ has caused a paradigm shift that calls for recalibrating all former commands in the light of his centrality. This approach recognizes that the law of Moses in its entirety has come to an end in the sense that the believer does not start by asking, "What did the law teach?" The believer begins at the point where his Christian life began: Christ. The believer found new life in Christ and so now comes to Christ to find out how to live out his new life.[9]

Without question, rule-of-life adherents would agree that the starting point must be Christ; but with their insistence that the law remains binding on Christians, one must ask whether the paradigm shift that Meyer points to as necessary has in fact occurred in their thinking.

What Paul is doing in all of the above instances where he employs the law is not putting the obligation of the Decalogue on believers, nor presenting it as rule, but rather, as Brian Rosner notes, he is reappropriating it as wisdom.

> On two occasions, in the midst of using the law for ethics, Paul attaches enlightening epithets to the law. When Paul uses the law for practical purposes as a pastor, it is not the law as "commandments," "books," "decrees," or "legal code" to which he appeals, but rather the law as "instruction" as in 1 Cor 10:11, and "teaching" as in Rom 15:4. These two texts reveal something of the apostle's

9. Meyer, *End of the Law*, 283.

hermeneutic when he reads the law for ethics. As it turns out, both are closely associated with wisdom.[10]

This distinction is critical to understand, for Paul continues to use the law and the entire Old Testament for wisdom, instruction, and prophecy, even while he sets aside the obligation of law as commandment for believers.

The two passages Rosner cites as examples are Romans 15:4 ("For whatever was written in former days was written for our instruction, that through endurance and through the encouragement of the Scriptures, we might have hope") and 1 Corinthians 10:11 ("Now these things happened to them as an example, but they were written down for our instruction, on whom the end of the ages has come"). These Scriptures provide a further illustration of what Paul affirmed at the end of Romans 3—that his doctrine upholds the law. It accords with the Old Testament revelation, and he in no way sets aside the record of God's faithfulness to the patriarchs. Nor is this use limited to the Decalogue. When speaking of payment for those in ministry, Paul cites Deuteronomy 25 as his evidence: "Let the elders who rule well be considered worthy of double honor, especially those who labor in preaching and teaching. For the Scripture says, 'You shall not muzzle the ox when it treads out the grain.'"[11] The apostle finds instruction and wisdom for believers now by reappropriating sections of the Torah in ways we sometimes don't expect.

Does this represent a strong law-gospel antithesis in Paul's thought? Indeed it does, but this is not the same as affirming a strong law-obedience antithesis. Horton affirms that

> "Law" as a principle simply refers to anything that God commands. Anything that comes to us from God in the form of imperatives (things to do or not do) is law. This can be in the form of the Ten Commandments, the elaborate specifications of the temple furnishings, Jesus's

---

10. Rosner, *Paul and the Law*, 184.

11. 1 Tim 5:17–18.

> teaching on divorce and remarriage, or instructions for
> life in the Spirit in Galatians 5:16–24.[12]

But this will not harmonize with Paul's teaching about the place of
his own instruction in contrast to the Mosaic law. He freely commands his converts in all manner of ways on what they must do,
and what they must refrain from doing, but he never equates his
Spirit-guided instruction with law. Here, too, we need to recall the
paradigm shift that Meyer referred to. With the death of Christ,
all has changed. As those under the headship of Christ, we now
receive apostolic teaching—indeed, have an obligation to it—not
the commands of law given to those in Adam.

The difference between keeping and fulfilling is similar to
the difference between one who is a native speaker of a language,
and one who has learned a language as a second tongue. The non-
native speaker must at times revert to thinking through the proper
way of forming words, and can at times speak haltingly, as they
may struggle over the language. For the native speaker, they do
not concentrate on keeping the rules of grammar, on conjugat-
ing verbs just so, or making sure they are speaking grammatically
correct. Rather, they speak naturally and without effort to adhere
to the rules. In so doing, they don't violate the rules of grammar,
but neither do they focus on them. Believers are native speakers of
grace. The righteous requirement of the law is fulfilled in them, but
not because they strive to keep the law.

The Sabbath

Christian tradition has interpreted the fourth commandment with
some degree of flexibility. If the Ten Commandments remain binding upon believers of all ages, how are we to treat this command? The
most common practice regards Sunday as the Sabbath and reshapes
the command to fit one's view of what one should or shouldn't do
on the day. But there are difficulties with this. Note that in Genesis
2, at the completion of creation, God blessed the seventh day, and

12. Horton, *God of Promise*, 174.

rested, but there is no command to Adam that he rest on this day. It is God who rested. When God introduces the Sabbath to Israel as part of the Decalogue, it then includes the prohibition on work, but not a lot of explanation. Only later, in Exodus 31, do we find a fuller pronouncement of the meaning of the Sabbath.

> You are to speak to the people of Israel and say, "Above all you shall keep my Sabbaths, for this is a sign between me and you throughout your generations, that you may know that I, the LORD, sanctify you. You shall keep the Sabbath, because it is holy for you. Everyone who profanes it shall be put to death. Whoever does any work on it, that soul shall be cut off from among his people. Six days shall work be done, but the seventh day is a Sabbath of solemn rest, holy to the LORD. Whoever does any work on the Sabbath day shall be put to death. Therefore the people of Israel shall keep the Sabbath, observing the Sabbath throughout their generations, as a covenant forever. It is a sign forever between me and the people of Israel that in six days the LORD made heaven and earth, and on the seventh day he rested and was refreshed."[13]

The Sabbath is Saturday, the seventh day of the week, and it remains so. There is often a free use of the word to designate Sunday as the Sabbath, when the church gathers for public worship. But this is a change from the biblical use. To regard Sunday as the Sabbath day isn't found in the New Testament. Without exception, Sunday is the Lord's Day. This designation comes from the day of his resurrection, but it is nowhere called the Sabbath. The Sabbath is also a sign between God and the nation of Israel. There is no reason to think this refers to anyone other than the physical seed of Jacob. God excludes the gentiles in this, and reserves the Sabbath as a covenant sign between himself and Jacob's posterity.

Michael Horton holds the rule-of-life position that the Ten Commandments are an obligation for believers today, but he does not include the Sabbath in this. He in fact relegates it to the ceremonial part of the law: "To suggest that the fourth commandment,

13. Exod 31:13–17.

then, is part of the *ceremonial*, rather than the *moral*, law is to say that it is no longer binding for Christians."[14] Horton goes on to cite reasons from the New Testament why the fourth commandment is unique among the Ten, including the fact that it cannot be credibly claimed that it is stamped on the human conscience, as the others are, and that it is nowhere repeated: "We search in vain to find one single New Testament commandment concerning the Sabbath."[15]

It is likewise noteworthy that the Sabbath in Israel was not a day of worship, but a day of rest. Indeed, there were certain feasts of the Lord that were sometimes called Sabbaths, but these are not the same as the weekly day of rest. The Day of Atonement occurred on the tenth day of the month. Exodus names this a Sabbath of solemn rest.[16] The association of Sabbath with worship among the Jews is likely tied to the rise of the synagogue. (Everett Ferguson notes that the origins of the synagogue are unknown; "More plausible theories refer to the time of the exile or the post-exilic period in gatherings for the reading and study of the law.")[17]

In the apostolic era, it was not the case that the first Christians began to think of Sunday as the replacement for the Sabbath. Mark F. Rooker says that

> Early church fathers such as Ignatius (35–107) and Barnabas (before AD 135) argued for exclusion of Sabbath observance, but they did not attempt to make Sunday the new Sabbath. Tertullian appears to be the first of the church fathers to suggest that business be deferred on Sunday so as to enhance worship, but still Sunday was a workday, not a day of rest . . . Following the fourth century, there was a steady move toward identifying the Sabbath with Sunday . . . Puritans such as Jonathan Edwards argued that, in light of the new covenant blessings in Christ, Sunday had replaced Saturday. According to the

---

14. Horton, *Law of Perfect Freedom*, 124.

15. Horton, *Law of Perfect Freedom*, 126.

16. Lev 23:26–32.

17. Ferguson, *Backgrounds of Early Christianity*, 539.

NT, there are no grounds for treating the Old Testament Sabbath as a continuing legal requirement for believers.[18]

The occurrences of the Sabbath in the New Testament either proclaim no need to observe the day (Rom 14:5, Col 2:16) or they highlight its significance as a type. The author of Hebrews refers to the Sabbath to say that it speaks of our rest in Christ, of ceasing from our labor to be right with God, and of trusting him. This accords with Horton's classification of it with the ceremonial part of the law, but it does raise the following questions: must believers today obey the Nine Commandments? Can we include the Sabbath in the moral law?

This is not to suggest that a rhythm of rest is not a good idea, or that Christians do not have freedom to treat a day as holy or set apart. Indeed they do, and that is the point—they may or they may not. As Paul counsels, "Each one should be fully convinced in his own mind,"[19] and we should not pass judgment on brothers or sisters who hold different convictions on the matter.[20] The Sabbath commandment identifies the difficulty in saying that the Ten Commandments are the summation of God's moral law, and remain binding on Christians today, while it is demonstrable from the New Testament that the earliest Christians had no such view of the Sabbath. It also shows how easy it is to incorporate culture and tradition into our treatment of the law, and to assume a biblical basis for practices where this is wanting. The New Testament does not present obligation to the Fourth commandment, but liberty and freedom. It is likewise clear that the Sabbath commandment is part of the Decalogue, and thus presents a difficulty for any claim of continuing obligation to the law.

18. Rooker, *Ten Commandments*, 98–99.
19. Rom 14:5.
20. Rom 14:10.

The Law Implanted in Christian Hearts

The book of Hebrews is an anonymous epistle, and though there has always been a desire to pin down the writer, the Holy Spirit has left this question unanswered. The majority of the evidence we've examined has come from Paul, but whether he is the author of Hebrews is not critical. The question is whether one can make a case for law in the new covenant from Hebrews. In chapter 8 of the epistle, the writer quotes extensively from Jeremiah 31, outlining the promises of God to initiate a new covenant with the house of Israel. The expiration of the old covenant is a key part of why the writer quotes this, for the citation is bookended by these two statements: "For if that first covenant had been faultless, there would have been no occasion to look for a second"[21] and "In speaking of a new covenant, he makes the first one obsolete."[22]

The challenge comes with verse 10: "For this is the covenant that I will make with the house of Israel after those days, declares the Lord: I will put my laws into their minds, and write them on their hearts, and I will be their God, and they shall be my people." Isn't this a clear statement of continuity of the law between the covenants; that the law in fact does remain in the new covenant? If the law as known in the old covenant is implanted into the hearts of new covenant believers, this raises questions of consistency. Would such an internalizing of the law include the whole of it? Must the sacrificial system be re-introduced, as well as keeping all the feasts of Jehovah?

Later in the book, the writer will outline the inability of animal sacrifices to take away sin. They were but a shadow of the good things to come. Now that Jesus has by his one sacrifice put away sin, these former sacrifices are removed: "For by a single offering he has perfected for all time those who are being sanctified."[23] And, indeed, among those who view it to be the old covenant law that is now put into the heart of believers, they limit this to the

21. Heb 8:7.
22. Heb 8:13.
23. Heb 10:14.

Decalogue, to what was written in stone at Sinai. No one suggests that God puts the dietary laws within the hearts of new covenant believers. Simon Kistemaker, for example, says that "God made the old covenant with the nation Israel and gave the people his laws written on tablets of stone. He establishes the new covenant with the believer in Christ and writes God's law on the believer's heart."[24] While it is true that the Decalogue was written in stone as the treaty document when Israel came out of Egypt, the citation from Jeremiah does not refer to the tablets. It is therefore untenable to suggest that this represents a reintroduction of the entire old covenant law, but on what basis would we say it refers only to the Ten Commandments?

Several writers prefer a view that affirms the law written on the hearts of believers, but as changed, radicalized, or "Christologized."[25] This seems but another way of saying, as Rosner does, that the law is used as wisdom. If it includes obligation to law, however, it ceases to be used in this way. A key to apostolic use of law is that it excludes obligation, even as Paul employs it for wisdom and prophecy. For the cross, as the central act in salvation history, has forever changed how new covenant believers relate to the law. Moreover, since the writer has made plain that the old covenant has ended, whatever is written on the heart of new covenant believers cannot be what belonged to the old covenant. It must be something different, something transformed. This is further underscored by Hebrews 8:9, where it says that the new covenant is "not like the covenant that I made with their fathers on the day when I took them by the hand to bring them out of the land of Egypt." That covenant, made at Sinai, was temporal, and its laws likewise were limited and not eternal statutes. Therefore, we cannot equate the law written on the heart of believers in the new covenant with the law at Sinai.

But didn't Jeremiah expect continuity? After all, the only law he knew was the one given at Sinai, so of course he would understand the prophecy to refer to the Ten Commandments. If

24. Kistemaker, *Hebrews*, 229.
25. Joslin, *Hebrews, Christ, and the Law*, 8.

Jeremiah did not see the full extent of this when God spoke to him, this is not at all surprising. Doubtless Hosea would have never imagined when he wrote "Out of Egypt have I called my son" that God did not refer only to Israel emerging from bondage, but that there would be yet another fulfillment of this prophecy when Jesus, Mary, and Joseph returned to Israel after fleeing from Herod to Egypt. The way in which New Testament writers quote and apply the Old Testament is often in ways we find surprising and unexpected.

Some argue, as Philip Hughes does, for the change in the believer, rather than any change in the law as responsible for what comes with the new covenant: "Though the Christian believer is not justified by the works of the law, but by the law-keeping and self-offering of Another on his behalf, yet the law of God is the standard of holiness required of him; only now he is enabled to love and obey the commandments of God which before he hated and disobeyed."[26] Indeed, there has been a change in the believer; that is, when someone comes to believe in Jesus, there are radical and profound changes, including their removal from being under Adam to now being under Christ. An associated change is that the standard of holiness required of believers in this age is not the Mosaic law, but Jesus himself. But nowhere does the New Testament describe the believer as enabled to keep the law. He is described as dead to the law, as released from it. Being dead to the law, Paul tells the Galatians, is in fact the way of living to God: "For through the law, I died to the law, so that I might live to God."[27] How, one may ask, can we go from this position of death to the law, to a position where the law is now our standard of holiness? Hughes reintroduces the old covenant statutes as part of the new covenant, but the context cannot support this. The new covenant is truly new, and thus what God implants in the hearts of Christians is also new. One may also take the implications of the implanted law to their logical conclusion. If the law is now written on the

26. Hughes, *Hebrews*, 301.

27. Gal 2:19.

hearts of believers (in whatever altered form), then the idea of an external rule, an imposed standard, ceases to make sense. Barry Joslin comments,

> In Hebrews 8, it is the law as viewed through the lens of Christ that is internalized—Christ becomes the interpretive principle and set of lenses through and by which the law must now be viewed in these eschatological "latter days." The law has been transformed in Christ, and this transformation involves both its internalization and its fulfillment in the New Covenant.[28]

While I concur with Joslin, I believe transformation may not fully capture what happens to the law in the new covenant. Here, too, Brian Rosner's observations are helpful. He notes that Paul explicitly replaces the law with Christ:

> Christians are not under the Law of Moses, but under the law of Christ, the law of faith, and the law of the Spirit. We have died to the law, Christ lives in us and we live by faith in the Son of God. Above all else, including righteousness under the law, we value knowing Christ Jesus our Lord. We do not keep the law, but fulfill the law in Christ and through love. We do not seek to walk according to the law, but according to the truth of the gospel, in Christ, in newness of resurrection life, by faith, in the light, and in step with the Spirit.[29]

The promised covenant of Hebrews 8 and Jeremiah 31 is a truly new covenant, not like the one at Sinai. Because of this, we should not look for what is implanted in the heart of believers to be the treaty stipulations of the old covenant. It is something different. If Jeremiah describes them as "law," this is understandable given his position in the timeline of salvation history. But it is clear that, to make sense of the new covenant, one must account for the other statements about law we've examined. Those statements make it impossible to see the Ten Commandments only as what God writes on the heart of believers in this age.

28. Joslin, *Hebrews, Christ, and the Law*, 134.

29. Rosner, *Paul and the Law*, 221–22.

6

As You Received Christ, Walk in Him

> *Paul never says, as he does of Jews, that believers in Christ rely on the law, boast about the law, know God's will through the law, are educated in the law, have light, knowledge and truth because of the law, do, observe, keep the law, on occasion transgress the law, or possess the law as letter or a written code, as a book, as decrees, or as commandments. Paul also never says, as he does of Jews, that Christians learn the law, walk according to the law, and expect good fruit and good works to flow from obedience to the law.*
>
> —Brian Rosner[1]

In Paul's instructions and exhortations to the churches, he consistently urges them to conform themselves to the Lord Jesus Christ. The way in which they entered God's family was by faith. The way they grow into Christ's image is by faith. The error he confronted in Galatia was an attempt to use the law to achieve this end. From apostolic times until now, it has been a perennial danger that we substitute law-keeping for life, doing rather than being. Our walk in newness of life does not need to be controlled by law, for the Spirit himself is our guide, and leads us into all truth. How,

1. Rosner, *Paul and the Law*, 221.

then, do we walk if we need not reference the law? Paul answers that, in several ways throughout the epistles, but his chief answer is "in him," meaning Christ. Exploring the richness of all that those two words contain is part of the practice of godliness and sanctification.

The Law of Christ and "en-lawed" to Christ

In the final chapter of Galatians, Paul makes the statement, "Bear one another's burdens, and so fulfill the law of Christ."[2] Some view this as a kind of rehabilitation of the Mosaic law, of Paul teaching that with the coming of the Spirit, the law can now at last be rightly understood—and rightly obeyed. One ground for this position is that because in every prior reference to the word "law" in Galatians, Paul has meant the Mosaic law; there would be no reason to think 6:2 is any different. J. Louis Martyn notes that "Gal 6:2 is the thirty-first of Paul's references in Galatians to *nomos* [law], and in all of the other significant instances the reference is to *the* Law."[3] Is this a confirmation for a continuing role of the Mosaic law, a proof that the law does indeed remain our standard in this age? For this to be true, Paul must have changed his position to suggest that the law is now a positive force in the Galatians' lives. Indeed, Martyn suggests that we should read it as the law of Moses, albeit "the Law as it has been taken in hand by Christ Himself."[4] In other words, the law as changed by Christ is now something different. This allows the apostle to use this term as a summation for their pursuit of godliness.

To maintain we must consistently define "law," as the Mosaic law introduces inconsistency in Paul's understanding of the law, its characteristics, and its effect on mankind. He assigned a purpose to the law in chapter 3 that limited it in time and purpose. If the arrival of faith has rehabilitated the Mosaic law for Christian living,

2. Gal 6:2.
3. Martyn, *Galatians*, 555.
4. Martyn, *Galatians*, 557.

he undercuts his previous constraints on the law belonging to a different age, and he reverses himself on the ability of the law to be a useful guide. As a rule of life, or a standard to which the Galatians should refer, Paul has been negative of the law throughout the entire epistle. He has warned and scolded, urging the Galatians not to accept a yoke of slavery. In other words, consistency dictates that we see in his view that the Mosaic law is unhelpful to the Galatians. If he now alters that position to suggest the law of Moses is something they should look to, he has left the Galatians unprepared for such a change. The only possible evidence for such a shift would be in chapter 5: "Do not use your freedom as an opportunity for the flesh, but through love serve one another. For the whole law is fulfilled in one word, you shall love your neighbor as yourself."[5] Even here, however, Paul says we arrive at fulfilling the law by love, not by the law itself! This is not an endorsement for the Mosaic law as a rule of life.

It is not so startling if Paul means something different with "the law of Christ" than he does with previous uses of the word: "The apostle who is capable of speaking of two covenants in Galatians, and of a new covenant in 2 Cor 3 is also perfectly capable of speaking of two different Laws."[6] Paul is using the term "law of Christ" differently than any previous use of the word. He has cautioned the Galatians on the impossibility of using the law alongside faith. He has said the law is not of faith, that Christians are not under the law, and he has contrasted the Spirit with the law. He said that through the law, he died to the law, so that he might live to God.

The Christian walks in the Spirit by faith, two things that belong to this present age. The law belongs to the prior age, where the pedagogue ruled. Since the arrival of faith, the pedagogue is gone. To use the Mosaic law as our guide in this age is, according to the apostle, incompatible with life in the Spirit. These contrasts make it unlikely to think of the law of Christ as the law of Moses, taken in hand by Christ. We pursue the imperative to love without

5. Gal 5:13–14.

6. Witherington, *Grace in Galatia*, 424.

reference to the law, without the agency of it. Indeed, as we love, as we prefer one another, we fulfill the law, but Paul has not told the Galatians to use the law to pursue love. He has said that the law's fulfillment will be a result of their pursuit of love.

Many view the law of Christ as a principle of selflessness, for Paul is speaking not of individuals keeping commands (note it is not keep, but fulfill the law of Christ), but of the way believers relate to one another, and the principle of self-sacrifice that the Lord Jesus Christ exemplified even to the point of death. Paul is keen to put before the Galatians the example of the Lord Jesus and his love for sinners. His sacrifice was the ultimate in burden-bearing when he took our sins upon himself at Calvary. The statement Paul made previously in 5:18, that if believers walk by the Spirit they are not under the law, represents a contrast between the law and the Spirit, not continuity. Ronald Fung notes that Paul "speaks of 'the law of Christ' polemically, if not almost playfully, as an antithesis to 'the law of Moses.' It is as though he said to his converts: if you must observe the law (as the agitators say), do so, only make sure that the law you observe is not Moses' law, but the law of Christ."[7] Betz concurs that "the unique position of the notion of 'law of Christ' makes it most likely that it is used here polemically."[8]

In using the phrase, Paul does not present the Mosaic law as the norm and standard for Christian conduct. As he has always done, he teaches that the law is not inconsistent with holiness, but it is not now the measure of it. In the new covenant community, the standard is the example of the Lord Jesus himself. Das, although he sees the law of Christ as a reference to the Mosaic law (redefined by Christ), says "By the Spirit's power the believer looks to and follows Christ's example. Then the requirements of the Mosaic Law will take care of themselves."[9] Paul never foregrounds the law in his instruction to believers in this age, but always backgrounds it. If we reverse this order, we are inconsistent with the apostolic treatment of law.

7. Fung, *Galatians*, 287–88.

8. Betz, *Galatians*, 301.

9. Das, *Paul and the Jews*, 172.

Even those who otherwise hold to the "third use" do not see a parallel to Moses here. Calvin says,

> There is an implied contrast between the law of Christ and the law of Moses, as if he said "If you desire to keep a law, Christ enjoins on you a law which you can only prefer to all others; and that is, to cherish kindness towards each other. He who lacks this has nothing." On the other hand, he says that when everyone compassionately helps his neighbor, the law of Christ is fulfilled.[10]

Howard F. Vos similarly comments, "The law of Christ may also be viewed as including all the self-sacrifice of Christ."[11] Leon Morris says, "This is not a law in the sense of part of a legal code, but it points to the necessity for lowly service if we would truly be followers of Jesus."[12] R. Longenecker notes,

> I propose that τὸν νόμον τοῦ χριστοῦ [the law of Christ] as does ἔννομος χριστοῦ [en-lawed to Christ of 1 Cor 9:21] stands in Paul's thought for those "prescriptive principles stemming from the heart of the gospel (usually embodied in the example and teachings of Jesus), which are meant to be applied to specific situations by the direction and enablement of the Holy Spirit, being always motivated and conditioned by love." Paul is not setting forth Jesus as a new Moses.[13]

Far from insisting on adherence to a legal code or to commandments of the old covenant, Paul is instead pressing the Galatian believers to embrace the example of Jesus in his love for mankind. It was not law that brought Jesus to earth in humility, to die in the place of sinners. Rather, it was love from beginning to end, in the eternal counsels of the Godhead, that caused the Father to send the Son. It was love that motivated the Son to come to earth and offer himself on the cross. What we read here in Galatians is consistent with the "new commandment" of John's gospel: "A new commandment I

10. Calvin, *Galatians*, 110.

11. Vos, *Galatians*, 111.

12. Morris, *Galatians*, 179

13. Longenecker, *Galatians*, 276

give to you, that you love one another: just as I have loved you, you also are to love one another." This is the kind of love that law does not consider. The law commanded love for others, and Leviticus 19 spells this out to be fellow Israelites, and even strangers (19:34), but it did not extend to one's enemies. The love of one's enemies was unique to the Lord Jesus, as Paul marvels in Romans 5: "For one will scarcely die for a righteous person—though perhaps for a good person one would dare even to die—but God shows his love for us in that while we were still sinners, Christ died for us."[14] This love surpasses anything in the law.

The apostle has also said the same to the Philippians as he does to the Galatians: "Let each of you look not only to his own interests, but also to the interests of others."[15] This is but the same command to fulfill the law of Christ, in different words, and Paul backs this up once again with the example of the Lord Jesus. His humiliation in coming to earth as a servant, and not only suffering death, but the death of the cross, was the establishment of the law of Christ. All this is motivation for Christian discipleship, for following after him. In other words, it is the Lord Jesus himself in his self-sacrificial character and life that are the believer's example, not the Mosaic law.

Consistent with the servant heart he tells the Galatians to model, Paul also reveals his own heart to the Corinthian believers. In chapter 9 of the first epistle, he speaks of three distinct groups he sought to win to Christ. These are Jews, those under law, and those outside the law. Jews are the seed of Jacob to whom the law was given ("to them belong the adoption, the glory, the covenants, the giving of the law").[16] But those "under law" are not themselves Jews. Rather, they are gentiles, for whom the Jewish way of life had an appeal, and who wished to join themselves to the Israelite community, and to live according to the precepts of the law. Cornelius the Centurion in Acts 10 appears to be such a man. F. F. Bruce comments on the words used to describe Cornelius ("one who

14. Rom 5:7–8.
15. Phil 2:4.
16. Rom 9:4.

feared God") as "generally used to denote those who, though not full proselytes, attached themselves to the Jewish religion, practicing its monotheistic and imageless worship, attending the synagogue, observing the Sabbath and food laws, etc."[17] To these Paul also preached (as did Peter to Cornelius). But the final group refers to those outside the law, and this refers to gentiles. But Paul adds this caveat to his explanation: "To those outside the law I became as one outside the law (not being outside the law of God but under the law of Christ) that I might win those outside the law."[18] Is Paul here putting himself under the law?

While admitting it cannot be the Mosaic law proper, some commentators seek to maintain the threefold distinction we have frequently encountered. Charles Hodge writes, "When among the Gentiles he did not conform to the Jewish law; in that sense, he was without law; but he did not act as without law to God, i.e., without regard to the obligation of the moral law."[19] Enough has been said about such divisions of law as artificial that it is clear no such distinction exists in the apostle's teaching. When he says he is "under the law of Christ," this is not an accurate translation. Rather, he terms himself "en-lawed to Christ" (*ennomos christou*). The word is unique in all of Paul's discussion about the law throughout his epistles. As C. K. Barrett says, the word "is not one that he ever uses of Jews, who were under the law."[20] This is wordplay on the part of the apostle. Gordon Fee comments,

> He wishes no misunderstanding of the word *anomos*, which would ordinarily mean to behave in a godless way. To be "as one without law" does not mean to be "lawless." As earlier ([1 Cor] 7:19) this is a clear instance in which Paul can distinguish between keeping "the law" and obeying the ethical imperatives of the Christian faith. For Paul the language "being under (or 'keeping') the law" has to do with being Jewish in a national-cultural-religious

17. Bruce, *Acts*, 215.

18. 1 Cor 9:21.

19. Hodge, *First Epistle to the Corinthians*, 165.

20. Barrett, *First Epistle to the Corinthians*, 213.

sense; but as a new man in Christ he also expects the Spirit to empower him (as well as all God's new people) to live out the ethics of the new age, which are the commands of God (7:19) now written on our hearts of flesh (cf. Ezek 36:26–27).[21]

When Paul uses this phrase, then, he is not putting himself (or believers) under the law, nor does it have any reference to the Mosaic law, except by way of contrast. Rather, Paul is specifying the personal relationship he has with the Lord Jesus. He is making a declaration of the sovereignty of Christ over his life, that he belongs to Jesus, is his bondservant, and that his ministry is just that—a service rendered to the one who owns him. Vine says that Paul "describes the intimacy of a relation and union established by the loyalty of a will devoted to Christ."[22] As a servant, he seeks to emulate his master in every way, and part of that emulation is to show Christ-like love to all. Being en-lawed to Christ "has a near parallel in Gal 6:2, where to 'bear one another's burdens' and in general to 'walk by the Spirit' amount to fulfilling the law of Christ."[23]

As Fee noted, however, the Christian faith does include ethical imperatives, and Paul's letters are filled with such instruction to his churches. But while local necessity required the apostle to address certain situations in various cities, the counsel and directives he provides are not exhaustive, covering every dilemma believers might face. As Longenecker notes,

> Even the definite command of the Lord regarding marriage is not considered by Paul to be "law" in the Jewish sense of a detailed code covering every exigency. Instead, it partakes of the nature of a principle; a principle which points the way to the solution in the particular circumstance but which must be applied anew to differing situations.[24]

21. Fee, *First Epistle to the Corinthians*, 430.

22. Vine, *I Corinthians*, 126–27.

23. Bruce, *1 and 2 Corinthians*, 88.

24. Longenecker, *Paul, Apostle of Liberty*, 174–75.

One can see this at work in what he writes to the Philippians. Describing his own pursuit of Christ, and conformity to him, he says "Let those of us who are mature think this way, and if in anything you think otherwise, God will reveal that also to you."[25] Paul has confidence that Spirit-led believers will grow and come to maturity. He need not present them with commands for every possible situation they may face.

One could collect all the apostolic instructions and summarily refer to them as "the law of Christ," but it would not alter the intention of Paul to present believers not with a code, but preeminently with a person. Renewing the mind, learning Christ, walking in love, and in the Spirit, indeed, putting on the Lord Jesus Christ, these are for Paul not less than the Decalogue. Rather, these things do what the law could not do; they transform believers into Christlikeness.

The ethical norms of the new covenant go beyond those of the old. We look to the person of Jesus in his self-sacrificial life as our pattern, not the commands of the old covenant. Is this a lower standard than what Moses spoke to the people of Israel at Sinai? On the contrary, the love demonstrated by the Son of God on a different mountain set for us the example of love that the Spirit puts before us. Indeed, as Paul tells the Corinthians, "what once had glory has come to have no glory at all, because of the glory that surpasses it."[26] The Mosaic law is not the final word on God's will for his people, for here we see in the law of Christ a standard rooted in love and in self-giving. It is not to Mount Sinai the believer looks, but to Mount Calvary.

Good Works in the Christian Life

In several places throughout Scripture, God seems almost to take us by the shoulders, look us in the eyes and say, "Holy living comes down to these few essentials." Verses such as Zechariah 7:9–10,

25. Phil 3:15.
26. 2 Cor 3:10.

"Thus says the LORD of hosts, render true judgments, show kindness and mercy to one another, do not oppress the widow, the fatherless, the sojourner, the poor, and let none of you devise evil against another in your heart," or Amos 5:14–15, "Seek good and not evil, that you may live, and so the LORD, the God of hosts, will be with you, as you have said. Hate evil and love good, and establish justice in the gate." These instructions all point to making our behavior match our belief; or to state it differently, because we are part of God's family, we should act like family members. When we come to the New Testament, here too we find similar statements: "This is the will of God, your sanctification," or "I urge you to walk in a manner worthy of the calling to which you have been called." These new covenant pronouncements are not in conflict with the old covenant desires. Rule-of-life adherents, then, have a point. God always desires his people to do good and avoid evil. A divergence comes when we ask, "How can we do the good?" The rule-of-life believer answers, "It has always been God's desire for his people to keep the Ten Commandments. If you do that, you're doing the good." But the New Testament shows that this answer is too simple. While we can say God wants his people practicing the good, what they do to reach this isn't defined in the New Testament by the Ten Commandments. When Paul refers to works, there are at least three different uses he employs when speaking of believers, and looking at each can provide an understanding of what his point is:

1. He refers to works as the summation of our stewardship throughout life, of all that God has entrusted to us. This use is (almost) confined to 1 Corinthians 3: "Each one's work will become manifest, for the Day will disclose it, because it will be revealed by fire, and the fire will test what sort of work each one has done."[27] Paul refers to the way believers have lived, how they have built on the foundation of Jesus Christ, and how their work will be tested in the coming judgment. This judgment is not to determine who possesses eternal life ("though he himself will be saved, but only as through fire"), but how Christians have tended to the trust com-

---

27. 1 Cor 3:13.

mitted to them in the gospel. When Paul says "each one's work," it is evident he is speaking of the total sum of all we have done. He speaks of the result of a life lived, but by the term "work" here he makes no comment on how a life is to be lived in God's service. Indeed, he draws a distinction between that which stands the test of fire (gold, silver, precious stones) and what will not endure it (wood, hay, straw), but both of these are collectively "each one's work." But Paul is here looking at a future evaluation of Christian stewardship, rather than giving guidance for now walking rightly. 1 Corinthians 3 isn't directly applicable to the question before us.

The "almost" qualification refers to Paul's statement in Romans 2:6: "He will render to each one according to his works." In this instance, again, he uses the word to refer to the summation of a life, but in this instance, a final judgment of life or death is in view. Paul is not teaching justification by works, but rather that the life course each of us follows displays and demonstrates in whom we trust. Those who have been born again will be followers of Jesus, and will by patience pursue the good. Those who do not trust him are those who do not obey the truth, and will not be found in the Book of Life.

2. Paul also refers to works as a description of deeds that conform to the law. In the first part of Romans, Paul indicted all mankind for their rebellion against God, and says in 3:20, "For by works of the law no human being will be justified in his sight, since through the law comes the knowledge of sin," and in verse 28, "For we hold that one is justified by faith apart from works of the law." In Romans 4, his examples of Abraham—"For if Abraham was justified by works"—and David—"God counts righteousness apart from works"—show that Paul sometimes interchanges "works" and "works of law." When he goes on to speak that the "promise did not come through the law," it is implicit that Paul means the promise does not come to those who do the works of the law. There is never any suggestion that those who keep the law would inherit righteousness.

In Galatians, Paul similarly affirms, "yet we know that a person is not justified by works of the law but through faith in Jesus

Christ, so we also have believed in Christ Jesus, in order to be justified by faith in Christ and not by works of the law, because by works
of the law no one will be justified."[28] In the following chapter, Paul
precludes any role for law whatsoever in our righteousness: "If a
law had been given that could give life, then righteousness would
have been by the law." Works, then, when spoken of in conjunction
with the law, are never presented positively. They always represent
a failed path to God, an autonomous attempt to justify oneself in
his sight. This is what Paul calls "another gospel" at the start of the
Galatian epistle, and which he so strongly condemns.

But it is likewise important to see that, not just at its com-
mencement by justification, but throughout the Christian life, the
apostle does not assign a helpful role to the law for believers. The
deeds that Paul describes as belonging to Christians cannot be
described as works of law, and in Paul's thinking they are fundamentally different than what the law requires.

3. Paul also refers to works, when qualified by the adjective
"good," as those acts that are descriptive of the behavior that should
characterize the redeemed. Paul uses the phrase "good works"
fourteen times, most often in the pastoral epistles. Believers, em-
powered by God's grace and his Spirit, are to "abound in every
good work."[29] Good works were prepared for believers to walk in
them.[30] We are to be fully pleasing to God, "bearing fruit in every
good work."[31] The rich in this world are to be generous, "rich in
good works."[32] As used by Paul, the term is linked to Christian behavior, but never to law. That is, believers are never told to pursue
good works by keeping the law. This is understandable if we recall
how the apostle uses "law" and "works of the law" as synonymous.

Paul gives two reasons for an incompatibility between the law
and good deeds. First, no one can keep the law, and the judgment
of the law on those who don't keep it is to condemn ("There is

28. Gal 2:16.
29. 2 Cor 9:8.
30. Eph 2:10.
31. Col 1:10.
32. 1 Tim 6:18.

none who does good, no not one"). Second, the purpose of the law was to reveal sin ("Through the law comes the knowledge of sin"). Even in the course of salvation history, when the Holy Spirit comes to indwell believers, Paul does not now employ the law as a tool of sanctification, nor suggest that we can achieve good works by reference to it. As he writes to Titus, "For the grace of God has appeared, bringing salvation for all people, training us to renounce ungodliness and worldly passions, and to live self-controlled, upright, and godly lives in the present age."[33] Grace, then, is the teacher of believers in this age, rather than law.

The later chapters of the Roman epistle are full of practical advice on how to actually live the Christian life. Romans 12:9–18 contains a set of staccato commands that Paul gives to the believers in that city. Here is a small sample:

> Let love be genuine. Abhor what is evil; hold fast to what
> is good. Love one another with brotherly affection. Outdo
> one another in showing honor. Do not be slothful in zeal,
> be fervent in spirit, serve the Lord. Rejoice in hope, be
> patient in tribulation, be constant in prayer. Contribute
> to the needs of the saints and seek to show hospitality.[34]

There is nothing here that contradicts the law, but there is much that goes beyond it. The Decalogue doesn't tell us to rejoice in hope, nor to be patient in tribulation. It doesn't tell us to outdo one another in showing honor. But one can discern here in Romans 12 the marks of humility, of that "mind of Christ" that Paul also told the Philippians should be in us. Apostolic commands, meant to conform believers to the person of Christ, are sufficient for the Spirit-indwelt Christian. Good works are uniquely Christian, and the result of the Spirit's work in us, conforming us to the image of God's Son.

33. Titus 2:11–12.

34. Rom 12:9–13

The Work of the Spirit

Throughout the first four chapters of Galatians, Paul has put before the Christians in that region the way of justification by faith, apart from works. His argument culminates in the first several verses of chapter 5 with a forceful plea against receiving circumcision which, despite being introduced with Abraham, had nevertheless come to signify adherence to the Mosaic law. But the apostle pivots from this important presentation of the ground of justification toward a discussion of their discipleship, of walking with Jesus. His instruction for following Jesus is the same as entering into a relationship with Jesus: by faith and apart from law. "But if you are led by the Spirit, you are not under law"[35] and "If we live by the Spirit, let us also walk by the Spirit."[36]

Here, again, is one of the contrasts that the apostle draws between law and the Spirit. Burton comments,

> life by the Spirit constitutes for the apostle a third way of life distinct both on the one hand from legalism and on the other from that which is characterised by yielding to the impulses of the flesh. It is by no means a middle course between them, but a highway above them both, a life of freedom from statutes, of faith and love.[37]

This makes an important point: Paul is not telling the Galatians that if they will but walk by the Spirit, the Spirit will help and empower them to keep the law. Common though it may be to believe that this is how the Spirit works holiness in us, this is not consistent with the apostolic doctrine. F. F. Bruce similarly writes,

> Here existence "under law" is antithetical to being "led by the Spirit" . . . With the coming of Christ and the completion of his redeeming work, the age of law has been superseded by the age of the Spirit. For the Galatians to retreat from grace to law would be to exchange

---

35. Gal 5:18.
36. Gal 5:24.
37. Burton, *Galatians*, 302.

the freedom of the Spirit for the bondage to the *stoicheia* [elementary principles].[38]

Near the end of the fifth chapter, Paul comes to a presentation of the way of the flesh and the way of the Spirit. This is one of his several "vice lists" that enumerates those works of the flesh that will end in spiritual death for its practitioners. He contrasts this with the fruit (not works) of the Spirit: "But the fruit of the Spirit is love, joy, peace, patience, kindness, goodness, faithfulness, gentleness, self-control; against such things there is no law."[39] Both lists tend less toward specific deeds and more toward attitudes (though, to be sure, there are deeds in the vice list). But he ends the first list by saying, "and things like these." It's as if Paul is saying to them, "the ways in which our sinful flesh can display itself are many—I'm simply giving you a few of the more obvious, but you and I both know there are many more." His prescription for overcoming such things is not "recall what the law says about this, and obey it." It is rather to "walk by the Spirit, and you will not gratify the desires of the flesh."[40]

Walking by the Spirit for Paul in fact precludes the law as commandments to obey. As Fee says, "The Spirit produces the fruit as believers continually walk with the Sprit's help. The essential nature of the fruit is the reproduction of the life of Christ in the believer."[41] That agrees with what Paul has told other congregations. He wrote to the Ephesians that if they walk the way unbelievers do, that would be inconsistent: "But that is not the way you learned Christ!—assuming that you have heard about him and were taught in him, as the truth is in Jesus."[42] Truth is found in a person, the one whom Paul preached. Keeping the law will not conform us to Christ, but being conformed to Christ will fulfill the law.

38. Bruce, *Galatians*, 245.
39. Gal 5:22–23.
40. Gal 5:16.
41. Fee, *Paul*, 114.
42. Eph 4:20–21.

The New Testament presents the example of the Lord Jesus and apostolic commands as guidance to believers, but his example and these commands are beyond the Mosaic law. They are not simply another form of law. How is it that such apostolic commands would not induce sin, as Paul claims the law does? The Spirit of God, indwelling believers, has inaugurated a new era in salvation history. This era is characterized by believers being "in Christ," as those who are associated with the heavenly, where Paul says we are seated with Christ. This realm is not associated with the Adamic nature, where Paul puts the law. Because of this, we can be free from condemnation but also obligation. The fatal weakness of the law is that it enjoined obligation but provided no transformation. Being in Christ comes with this transformation through the agency of the Holy Spirit. Paul consistently addressed "antinomian" concerns, not by telling believers that they were walking out of step with the law, but that they were not walking as Christ walked and as he himself had instructed them.

The fruit of the Spirit, like the vices, consists of attitudes we display, which will no doubt work themselves out in specific deeds and words. But Paul leaves that to the work of the Spirit within these believers, confident that if they will walk by the Spirit (and not by law), they will know how to please God. In the several places where Paul addresses conduct, he almost always describes attitudes and postures of the heart. To the Ephesians, again, he writes, "I therefore, a prisoner for the Lord, urge you to walk in a manner worthy of the calling to which you have been called, with all humility and gentleness, with patience, bearing with one another in love, eager to maintain the unity of the Spirit in the bond of peace."[43] These heart changes are what transform and conform us to the Lord Jesus. And nowhere is the law the instrument of accomplishing this transformation.

Concerning the fruit of the Spirit, Barrett says, "All are the consequence of the self-forgetfulness that looks away from itself to God. The Spirit which affects this disregard of self is in no sense

---

43. Eph 4:1–3.

legal, still less legalistic; yet in its effect it is entirely moral."[44] In other words, law cannot accomplish victory over self and sin, but the victory that comes through walking by the Spirit will fulfill the law and its requirement of holiness. It will not lead to antinomianism (much less lawlessness), but the cruciform shape of discipleship that characterizes New Testament believers. Paul ends the list of the Spirit's fruit with an ironic comment: "Against such things there is no law." This is doubtless a last jab at his opponents in the letter, those who had sought to bring the Galatian Christians under law. He says in effect, "You want law? Try this; no law against these things!" Barrett calls this "an ad hominem dig . . . you want to observe the law, don't you? You will not find any law that forbids these things."[45]

---

44. Barrett, *Freedom and Obligation*, 77.
45. Barrett, *Freedom and Obligation*, 77.

Epilogue

IN THE PREVIOUS CHAPTERS, I've examined positions on the Mosaic law and concluded that setting the law as the standard or rule of life is not sustainable from the New Testament evidence. I refer to this position as "hyponomianism," for the Greek preposition *hypo*, meaning under. While this hyponomian view affirms freedom from condemnation, it likewise presents the believer as still under law as a rule of life and conduct. For all the reasons presented, I do not believe this represents the true position of the Christian's relationship to law in the New Testament. We may note as well that the word "hyponomian" does in fact occur in the New Testament, when Paul tells the Romans, "sin will not have dominion over you, for you are not under law [*hyponomos*], but under grace." To transliterate, Paul says, "You are not hyponomian."

The other position that remains a popular foil is antinomianism. Considered in its components, the word means "against the law." At times, it is a caricature meaning complete absence of any moral standard or obligation. (Notably, the term does not occur in the New Testament.) Moreover, I know of no one who espouses such a position. Antinomianism is a straw man in discussions about the law. It is a false dichotomy to assert either that we must have the law as our standard or that we embrace antinomianism. The label "antinomian" means (in its most polemical manifestations) that one cares nothing for holiness, or for growth in sanctification. This, too, is a position I reject. But it isn't the case that there are only two choices in dealing with the biblical evidence. Some may present it that way, but the texts in question have called for a far more thorough examination, and have yielded a more subtle answer.

The New Testament presents an obligation to pursue Christlikeness, and clearly asserts that growth into his image is something every Christian must pursue. But the law is not an aid in reaching that goal. Due to our Adamic heritage, the vestiges of which are still within us, we cannot respond rightly to the law, even when indwelt by the Holy Spirit, and it serves not to make us holier, but to reveal sin. To repeat, it is diagnostic but not therapeutic. To see this from the way in which the apostle Paul speaks of law in his epistles is not antinomianism. It is often the case that a particular view of law comes as a part of a theological package, a system. Theological grids can be helpful, and frameworks for understanding Scripture are often effective ways to gain a better understanding of truth and doctrine. But we have to test our seams and see if they hold water. We learn from previous ages—indeed, we owe profound debts to earlier thinkers who clarified and uncovered long-forgotten or misunderstood truths—but we owe primary allegiance not to confessions or tradition, but to the canon of Scripture.

Nor is a rejection of obligation to law a denigration of the Old Testament as Christian Scripture. On the contrary, every part of the Hebrew Bible is God's word, and it is God's word for us today. When Paul wrote to Timothy, "from childhood you have been acquainted with the sacred writings, which are able to make you wise for salvation through faith in Christ Jesus," he was referring to the Old Testament. Paul uses these Scriptures to teach and admonish, and draws wisdom from them. Having reverence for the Old Testament as God's revelation does not mean we do not likewise recognize a new era in salvation history.

Were I to give a word to the position I am advocating (a position by no means unique or original from me) it may be that "exonomianism" best expresses it (*exo* = outside + *nomos* = law). The Christian's position as crucified with Christ, risen with him, and seated with him in the heavenly places puts us outside the realm and jurisdiction of the law. This is not the same as saying believers have no obligation to holiness. Indeed, we are en-lawed to Christ, under obligation to him. But we are not under Mosaic law in any way, neither for righteousness, nor for growth in holiness and sanctification. To be clear, the law did not die. It is still very much alive and active. Rather, when we died with Christ, were raised with him, and seated with him in the heavenly places, that new identity removed us from the law's dominion and jurisdiction. The man who has been executed has borne the full weight of the law's penalty. He cannot be executed a second time. We are in such a position, because Christ died in our place, and because his death is reckoned as ours, any former relationship with the law has ended.

If exonomianism is being outside the law's jurisdiction, we can liken the law to a pursuer, and believers are like those who have crossed over a river. The law stands on the opposite shore, crying out and shaking its fist at us for our failure to keep it. "You are talking to the wrong man!" we shout back. "All on your side of the shore are in Adam, and they alone are under your jurisdiction. I am on this side of the river, in Christ, and I have no more relationship to you. Besides, even those who are under your jurisdiction don't keep it. Have you any ability to enable obedience?" The law stands scowling, arms at its side, making no answer. For the law knows that it cannot enable obedience to any of its precepts in the sons of Adam, and that it has nothing to say to those in Christ. They have a higher standard and, critically, are indwelt by a Spirit that enables them.

Imagine that the river is the border between two countries and the picture becomes even clearer. The laws of one nation apply in that nation, but if we are outside of its borders, they do not. This is the exonomian position. We are outside the law's jurisdiction. Its threats and demands, and its condemnation, can do nothing to us. Holy and good though it is, we are unholy and evil, and the combination is a toxic one. Having crossed over this river, being on the other side, we are as good as dead to the law's demands. If we fail to understand our death to the law, we likely will fall into one of three traps. First, if we are honest about it, we will despair at our utter inability to keep the law, knowing that if we offend in one point, we are lawbreakers, plain and simple. Second, if we do have a good run at keeping the law, we will inevitably pat ourselves on the spiritual back, happy at our successful efforts, and be further persuaded that God himself must be happy with our performance. This only makes use proud and feeds our flesh. Third, we are apt to become hypocrites. Since we cannot keep the law's demands, our temptation will be to diminish them and to rationalize that surely God understands we are only human and he can't expect us to keep the law all the time. As McQuilken earlier noted, we keep it, but never perfectly. Is it using the law lawfully to treat it in this way? Is it upholding the law?

Someone may fairly ask the question of whether we're all getting to the same result. Are those who advocate a rule-of-life view, and those who hold the position I have presented, all coming to the same conclusion? If the Ten Commandments are consistent with God's will for believers now, does it really matter what the instrument of our growth is, as long as we grow? If the focus of our sanctification is the Ten Commandments, and the exhortation to be conformed to Christ rests on the Decalogue, we have missed the point. We do not embrace our position in Christ, and we do not reach the apostolic goal to "put on the Lord Jesus Christ." The identity of heavenly-seated believers in this age of grace is bound up with the exalted Christ. The law has nothing to add to him. The Spirit-indwelt believer has as his example the person of Christ, and the energy behind our transformation is grace through and through. The difference may be summarized most clearly by Westerholm: "When Paul speaks of Christian's 'fulfilling' the law, he is describing, not prescribing, their behavior. When Paul *prescribes* what Christians are to do, the language used is not that of fulfilling the Mosaic law: 'Walk by the Spirit, and do not gratify the desires of the flesh' ([Gal] 5:16, cf. Rom 8:12–13)." Naturally it is from Paul's prescriptions that we must derive his view of the basis for Christian obligation."[1] Stated differently, if we make it our

1. Westerholm, *Perspectives*, 434–35.

aim to keep the law, we can fall short of Christian maturity and conformity to Christ. If we make conformity to Christ our aim, we need not worry about fulfilling the law.

Those who do hold to a continuing obligation for the Decalogue today don't in fact live this way. They live as "exonomians," as those freed from the law. They are not living in dread of breaking God's laws, are not fearful of falling under his wrath for not keeping all of them. Thus someone such as A. W. Pink, who insists we must retain every jot and tittle, was himself not doing so.

Inherent in the rule-of-life position is a provision for fulfilling and setting aside a large part of the law. Dividing the law into its various categories is a kind of backdoor way to achieve freedom from obligation to it. Two out of the three traditional divisions are now set aside, and only the moral law remains. Yet here, too, it's not all the moral commandments, but just the Decalogue—and even the fourth commandment is frequently treated as ceremonial.

But it doesn't end there. Obligation to the Ten Commandments is really just a suggestion; for part of this view is also that there is no condemnation for the lawbreaker. Because of that, those who hold the rule-of-life view are in fact using the law for wisdom, reappropriating it, and viewing it differently than law— yet at the same time claiming that believers are obligated to keep it. They stop short of replacing the law with Christ, as the New Testament does, and because of that, the effect is a kind of spiritual dissonance. Free, yet not free. Thus they can offer only partial deliverance, and partial deliverance still involves some amount of mixture of the old covenant into the new covenant. Inconsistencies and perils therefore remain. I will identify three:

1. By insisting on law as an obligation, some Christians will feel nothing but a troubled conscience and lack of peace. The honest believer will fall short of the standard in the law, and if he is not grounded in the acceptance based solely on the blood of Christ, peace is fleeting, and such a one is not able to enjoy the life of faith in Jesus. A person of this mindset frets at their continual failure, and can become exceedingly performance-oriented. This is the condition into which Martin Luther fell, bringing his confessor to

exasperation when he would go on and on confessing his sins. That mindset can afflict us still. It's a good day if I've kept the law, and haven't messed up badly. But is this where the New Testament puts the emphasis on life in Christ? Is it not rather that we are to enjoy him, to thank him and praise him for redeeming such sinful and disobedient people as we are?

2. It can delude us to redefine sin downward. From time to time, I've noted the Wesleyan (Arminian) position that also holds to the rule-of-life view. There are within this tradition those who believe we can achieve sinlessness here on earth. If we limit sin to what we do or say alone, perhaps that would be true. But the thoughts of our hearts, the attitudes, and our unspoken anger and lust are likewise sin. And who among us would say that they never have an angry thought, are never selfish in their demeanor toward others, indeed that they do not fall short of this higher standard set forth for New Covenant believers?

Restricting sin to outward manifestations alone can trick us into thinking we have achieved some higher life, some holiness that is in fact based on our behavior. But this is a dangerous thing, because it, too, directs our eyes inward, toward our conduct and ourselves. Are we not to look carefully how we walk, as Paul tells the Ephesians? We are, certainly. But it is a great temptation to see ourselves as better than our fellow believers, as achieving a higher holiness because we are outwardly conforming to the law's demands. This is not putting on the Lord Jesus Christ.

3. It is apt to create a delusion that by keeping God's law we are progressing in holiness. As the many examples have shown, the standard and the mark we are to strive for is Christlikeness, not law-likeness. Jesus kept the law perfectly, but he did more than this. This "something more" is what he calls believers to. One may not be a murderer, but Jesus raised the bar much higher in saying that we should not hate, and in fact should love even our enemies! We can keep the law, but not fulfill it, and if we stop there, satisfied that we have done what God desires of us, we have deluded ourselves. Aside from this is the fact that, as the apostle has clearly shown, no man does or can keep the law. My faltering

adherence to the old covenant treaty would only condemn me, as it condemns any and all who do not keep it. For the one who has a good run at law-keeping, the result is apt to be pride, and further self-delusion. Luther himself lamented the difficulty of this: "I myself have been preaching and cultivating it [faith alone] through reading and writing for almost twenty years and still I feel the old clinging dirt of wanting to deal so with God that I may contribute something, so that he will have to give me his grace in exchange for my holiness."[2] If we are looking to a statute for God's approbation, rather than to the Savior himself, we are in fact setting aside the very one whom he has told us to watch.

What, then, is using the law lawfully? There are several observations we can make about the law and its place in the Christian life. As I've tried to make clear, the law in its broadest sense encompasses the whole Old Testament, and is God's word through and through. It is the inspired record of God's dealings with his people. All of God's word is instructive for God's people, even if we discern that some parts of it are not directly applicable to us now. We should reject the position of Marcion, an early heretic who, because he could not reconcile in his own mind the ways of God in the Old Testament with those of the New Testament, discarded the Hebrew Bible entirely. The hundreds of citations that the New Testament makes of the Old Testament should alone demonstrate the error of such a view. The Old Testament has a witnessing role in the gospel; as Paul says, "The gospel was preached to Abraham."

There are other ways in which the lack of knowledge and meditation on the law leaves us theologically impoverished. The fourth commandment, though not a command for the believer today, is nevertheless a powerful signpost of our rest in Christ. The physical rest required by the fourth commandment points forward to our spiritual rest in Christ. Those who trust in Jesus have entered into God's rest. Because of the unified nature of God's law, we can also say that the entire Pentateuch bears witness to Jesus. The sacrificial system, the tabernacle, the feast days—all these are types of the Lord Jesus. This is all "law" in the definition Jesus gives

2. *LW* 51:284.

to the disciples in Luke 24 on the Emmaus road. Knowledge of this part of God's word is vital to a proper understanding of the gospel, for it is all preparatory for the advent of Jesus. Think also of the ways in which the New Testament refers to and uses the Mosaic law. Consider once more Jesus' repeated statements in the Sermon on the Mount—"you have heard it said." His teaching takes it for granted that his hearers have heard it said. Jesus is making a comparison based on a known standard among the people, and the contrast—"but I say to you"—depends on their knowledge and understanding of the old covenant law.

In this narrower sense of the law as commandment, we can also see God's faithfulness to Israel. He brought them out of Egypt and gave them his law. The treaty he presented at Sinai served a dual purpose, even if only partially known by the people at that time. It marked them off as God's people, distinguishing them from the nations around them. They were to be different because God is different. But the law also bore witness to the people's inability to keep it. It served a purpose in salvation history that pointed to its own temporality. The law was added to increase transgressions, to shine the spotlight so brightly on sin that no one could claim any righteousness of their own. Paul tells the Romans that God was patient in passing over sins previously committed. That is, he held the penalty of those sins as if it were in escrow, until the death of Jesus. At that time, the only acceptable payment for sins was rendered, and God accepted the death of Jesus as payment, not just for past sins, committed under the era of law, but for future sins as well.

The law still serves this function of revealing sin. It is a boundary between good and evil, between right and wrong, that demonstrates to all mankind that they fall short. This is a lawful use of the law. When combined with our sinful nature, it still provokes sin, makes us want to do what it prohibits, and—rightly understood—should cause us to admit our guilt and inability to ever do right apart from becoming new creatures in Christ. In short, the law demonstrates the need for the Holy Spirit in our lives. We can see the consistent holiness of God throughout all of Scripture, and in the ways he has directed his people throughout history. In the Old Testament, it was through his law; in the New Testament, it is through his Spirit, directing us to Christ. But though the apostles will frequently cite the Old Testament law as supporting their teaching, their teaching just as frequently goes beyond what the law enjoins. This, too, presupposes a knowledge of and familiarity with God's law. But the constant message of the New Testament is that the Lord Jesus himself is now the standard, the one in whom we delight, and who is our pattern in every way. His fulfillment of the law through his death is what has brought us life—and freedom. The imperatives of the New Testament rest not on obligation to the law of Moses, but identification with the risen Christ.

Two things remain definitive in the way Paul treats the law, and these points are the touchstone for how Christians should regard it. Firstly, Paul consistently assigns the law to a prior age, and to the prior covenant. The promise preceded the law, and remains after the law has been fulfilled. The law was temporal in nature, never intended by God to be the ultimate standard for Christians. Paul's explanation of the law's purpose in Galatians makes this clear: "Now that faith has come, we are no longer under a guardian."[3] One cannot claim we are obligated to the law, and at the same time say we are no longer under a guardian. A failure to see this is a failure to distinguish God's purposes in salvation history. Indeed, Paul teaches nothing that contradicts the Law/Torah in its fullest sense. He upholds the law, but he recognizes the death and resurrection of Christ as the fulfillment of law. The law has not been made useless; it has been completed. Because it has been completed, and Christ is the end of the law for righteousness, Paul regards it in its proper eschatological sphere. It is part of God's revelation, a record of his faithfulness to Israel, a way to reveal and expose sin, but it no longer commands believers. It is still illustrative, and on occasion Paul will reference it as a springboard for his own exhortation, but he will not tell Christians the law is the substance of their obedience to God.

3. Gal 3:25.

Secondly, our identification with the risen Christ has fundamentally altered our relationship to the law, so that Paul speaks of Christians as having died to and being released from the law. Because the law belongs to the old covenant, it is not the instrument of new covenant holiness. Paul's appeal to Christians is that, because they have been raised up and seated with Christ, they should seek those things that are above. The law does not fit this description, but Paul's own instructions do. When he tells the Romans to "put on the Lord Jesus Christ, and make no provision for the flesh," this comes at the end of a long series of apostolic commands that express the character of the Lord Jesus, but commands that can't be found in the Mosaic code. "Bless those who persecute you; bless and do not curse them. Rejoice with those who rejoice, weep with those who weep. Live in harmony with one another. Do not be haughty, but associate with the lowly. Never be wise in your own sight. Repay no one evil for evil, but give thought to do what is honorable in the sight of all."[4] In this and other New Testament passages, the mind of Christ is put before the believer as the goal.

Christians have understandably struggled to make sense of the whole picture of their relationship to the law in this age of grace. It is, in a sense, a package. Bringing elements that properly belong to the old covenant into the new will lead to confusion and inconsistency. Similarly, if we understand all that God has done in the resurrection and seating us with Christ in the heavenly places, we will see that becoming more like what we already are is not accomplished by applying law to our lives. My plea is that Christians embrace what comes with their realm change, their heavenly citizenship, and their status as raised anew with Christ. We sometimes imagine we need to put up guardrails, fences, and walls by which Christians will know how to walk in a manner pleasing to God. Paul doesn't use the law for this. Indeed, this was the crux of the argument with the agitators in Galatia. They were bringing in the law and seeking to apply it to the lives of Christians, but Paul did not countenance it or concede that we need some control on our behavior beyond the Spirit. He tells them, "A little leaven leavens

4. Rom 12:14–17.

the whole lump." Any admixture of law with their walk in the Spirit would have a corrupting influence on the Galatians, Paul says.

As we received Christ Jesus (apart from the law, and through the witness of the Spirit), we are to walk in him. The basis of our sanctification is the same as that of our justification. Out of our identify flows our living and conduct. When we fall short, the answer is not a bit of law to correct us, but to recall who we are in Christ. The indwelling Holy Spirit directs believers to the person of Jesus, rather than old covenant precept, to the Savior rather than statute. If we look to him, we have all we need to become more like him.

Bibliography

Alford, Henry. *Alford's Greek Testament: An Exegetical and Critical Commentary.* Grand Rapids: Baker, 1980.

Althaus, Paul. *The Theology of Martin Luther.* Translated by Robert C. Schultz. Philadelphia: Fortress, 1966.

Barnhouse, Donald Grey. *Expositions of Bible Doctrines: Taking the Epistle to the Romans as a Point of Departure.* Vol. 3. Fincastle, VA: Scripture Truth, 1952.

Barrett, C. K. *The First Epistle to the Corinthians.* New York: Harper & Row, 1968.

————. *Freedom and Obligation: A Study of the Epistle to the Galatians.* Philadelphia: Westminster, 1985.

Bayes, Jonathan F. *The Weakness of the Law: God's Law and the Christian in New Testament Perspective.* Eugene, OR: Wipf & Stock, 2006.

Berkhof, Louis. *Manual of Christian Doctrine.* Grand Rapids: Eerdmans, 1933.

Bertone, John A. *"The Law of the Spirit": Experience of the Spirit and Displacement of the Law in Romans 8:1–16.* SiBL 86. New York: Peter Lang, 2007.

Betz, Hans Dieter. *Galatians: A Commentary on Paul's Letter to the Churches in Galatia.* Philadelphia: Fortress, 1988.

Bird, Michael F. *Romans.* SGBC 6. Grand Rapids: Zondervan, 2016.

Boice, James Montgomery. *Romans, Volume 2: The Reign of Grace (Romans 5:1—8:39).* Grand Rapids: Baker, 1991.

Bring, Ragnar. *Commentary on Galatians.* Translated by Eric Herbert Wahlstrom. Philadelphia: Muhlenberg, 1961.

Bruce, F. F. *1 and 2 Corinthians.* NCBC 49. London: Oliphants, 1971.

————. *The Book of Acts.* NICNT. Grand Rapids: Eerdmans, 1986.

————. *The Epistle to the Galatians: A Commentary on the Greek Text.* NIGTC 2. Grand Rapids: Eerdmans, 1982.

Burton, Ernest DeWitt. *A Critical and Exegetical Commentary on the Epistle to the Galatians.* ICC 35. Edinburgh, UK: T. & T. Clark, 1921.

Calvin, Jean. *The Epistles of Paul the Apostle to the Galatians, Ephesians, Philippians and Colossians.* Calvin's Commentaries 11. Edited by David W. Torrance and Thomas F. Torrance. Translated by T. H. L. Parker. Grand Rapids: Eerdmans, 1965.

————. *The Epistles of Paul the Apostle to the Romans and to the Thessalonians.* Calvin's Commentaries 8. Edited by David W. Torrance and Thomas F. Torrance. Translated by Ross Mackenzie. Grand Rapids: Eerdmans, 1960.

————. *Institutes of the Christian Religion.* Edited by John T. McNeill. Translated by Ford Lewis Battles. Philadelphia: Westminster, 1960.

————. *The Second Epistle of Paul the Apostle to the Corinthians and the Epistles to Timothy, Titus and Philemon.* Calvin's Commentaries 10. Edited by David W. Torrance and Thomas F. Torrance. Translated by T. A. Smail. Grand Rapids: Eerdmans, 1976.

Chamblin, Knox. "The Law of Moses and the Law of Christ." In *Continuity and Discontinuity: Perspectives on the Relationship Between the Old and the New Testaments: Essays in Honor of S. Lewis Johnson, Jr.,* edited by John S. Feinberg, 181–202. Westchester, IL: Crossway, 1988.

Cranfield, C. E. B. *A Critical and Exegetical Commentary on the Epistle to the Romans.* ICC 32a. 6th ed. Edinburgh, UK: T. & T. Clark, 1975.

Das, A. Andrew. *Galatians.* Concordia Commentary: A Theological Exposition of Sacred Scripture. St. Louis: Concordia, 2014.

————. *Paul and the Jews.* Peabody, MA: Hendrickson, 2003.

————. *Paul, the Law, and the Covenant.* Peabody, MA: Hendrickson, 2001.

Dorsey, David. "The Law of Moses and the Christian: A Compromise." JETS 34 (1991) 321–34.

Dunn, James D. G. *Romans.* WBC 38a. Dallas: Word, 1988.

English Standard Version Study Bible. Wheaton, IL: Crossway, 2011.

Erskine, John. "The Nature of the Sinai Covenant." In *Theological Dissertations,* 1–65. London: Maxwell and Wilson, 1809.

Fee, Gordon D. *1 and 2 Timothy, Titus: A Good News Commentary,* edited by W. Ward Gasque. New York: Harper and Row, 1984.

————. *The First Epistle to the Corinthians.* Grand Rapids: Eerdmans, 1987.

————. *Paul, the Spirit, and the People of God.* Peabody, MA: Hendrickson, 1996.

————. *Pauline Christianity: An Exegetical-Theological Study.* Peabody, MA: Hendrickson, 2007.

Ferguson, Everett. *Backgrounds of Early Christianity.* 2nd ed. Grand Rapids: Eerdmans, 1993.

Fisher, Edward. *The Marrow of Modern Divinity.* Philadelphia: Presbyterian Board of Publication, 1800.

Fung, Ronald Y. K. *The Epistle to the Galatians.* NICNT. Grand Rapids: Eerdmans, 1988.

Furnish, Victor Paul. *Theology and Ethics in Paul.* Louisville: Westminster John Knox, 2009.

Gaffin, Richard B. *By Faith, Not by Sight: Paul and the Order of Salvation.* 2nd ed. Phillipsburg, NJ: P. & R., 2013.

Gentry, Peter John, and Stephen J. Wellum. *Kingdom through Covenant: A Biblical-Theological Understanding of the Covenants.* Wheaton, IL: Crossway, 2012.

Gersh, Harry. *The Sacred Books of the Jews.* New York: Stein and Day, 1972.

Godet, Frédéric Louis. *Commentary on Romans*. Translated by Alexander Cusin. Grand Rapids: Kregel, 1977.

Gordon, T. David. "Abraham and Sinai Contrasted in Galatians 3:6–14." In *The Law Is Not of Faith: Essays on Works and Grace in the Mosaic Covenant*, edited by Bryan D. Estelle et al., 240–58. Phillipsburg, NJ: P. & R., 2009.

Grant, F. W. *The Numerical Bible*. Neptune, NJ: Loizeaux Brothers, 1892.

Green, Bradley G. *Covenant and Commandment: Works, Obedience, and Faithfulness in the Christian Life*. NSBT. Downers Grove: InterVarsity, 2014.

Griffith-Thomas, W. H. *St. Paul's Epistle to the Romans: A Devotional Commentary*. Grand Rapids: Eerdmans, 1986.

Haas, Guenther H. "Calvin's Ethics." In *The Cambridge Companion to John Calvin*, edited by Donald McKim, 93–105. Cambridge Companions to Religion. Cambridge: Cambridge University Press, 2004.

Harline, Craig. *Sunday: A History of the First Day from Babylonia to the Super Bowl*. New York: Doubleday, 2007.

Hodge, Charles. *A Commentary on the First Epistle to the Corinthians*. London: Banner of Truth Trust, 1958.

Hoekema, Anthony A. "The Reformed Perspective." In *Five Views on Sanctification*, edited by Stanley N. Gundry, 59–90. Counterpoints. Grand Rapids: Zondervan, 1987.

Hogg, C. F., and W. E. Vine. *The Epistle to the Galatians: With Notes Exegetical and Expository*. London: Pickering & Inglis, 1921.

Holwerda, David E. *Jesus and Israel: One Covenant or Two?* Grand Rapids: Eerdmans, 1995.

Horton, Michael Scott. *God of Promise: Introducing Covenant Theology*. Grand Rapids: Baker, 2006.

———. *The Law of Perfect Freedom*. Chicago: Moody, 1993.

Hughes, Philip Edgcumbe. *A Commentary on the Epistle to the Hebrews*. Grand Rapids: Eerdmans, 1977.

Joslin, Barry. *Hebrews, Christ, and the Law: The Theology of the Mosaic Law in Hebrews 7:1—10:18*. Paternoster Biblical Monographs. Milton Keynes, UK: Paternoster, 2008.

Kaiser, Walter C., Jr. "The Law as God's Guidance for the Promotion of Holiness." In *Five Views on Law and Gospel*, edited by Stanley N. Gundry, 177–99. Counterpoints. Grand Rapids: Zondervan, 1996.

———. "Leviticus 18:5 and Paul: Do This You Shall Live (Eternally?)." *Journal of the Evangelical Theological Society* 14 (1971) 19–28.

Kistemaker, Simon J. *New Testament Commentary: Exposition of the Epistle to the Hebrews*. Grand Rapids: Baker, 1984.

Kolb, Robert, et al., eds. *The Book of Concord: The Confessions of the Evangelical Lutheran Church*. Minneapolis: Fortress, 2000.

Kruse, Colin G. "Paul, the Law, and the Spirit." In *Paul and His Theology*, edited by Stanley E. Porter, 109–30. Leiden, Netherlands: Brill, 2006.

Lloyd-Jones, Martin. *Romans, An Exposition of Chapters 7.1—8.4: The Law, Its Functions and Limits.* Grand Rapids: Zondervan, 1974.

Longenecker, Bruce W. *The Triumph of Abraham's God: The Transformation of Identity in Galatians.* Nashville: Abingdon, 1998.

Longenecker, Richard N. *Galatians.* WBC 41. Dallas: Word, 1990.

————. *Paul, Apostle of Liberty.* Grand Rapids: Baker, 1976.

Luther, Martin. *Luther's Works.* Edited by Jaroslav Pelikan et al. 75 vols. St. Louis: Concordia, 1955–present.

MacArthur, John. *Ephesians.* The MacArthur New Testament Commentary. Chicago: Moody, 1986.

Macpherson, John, ed. *The Westminster Confession of Faith.* Edinburgh, UK: T. & T. Clark, 1882.

Martyn, J. Louis. *Galatians.* AB 33a. New Haven: Yale University Press, 2010.

McQuilkin, Robert Crawford. *God's Law and God's Grace.* Grand Rapids: Eerdmans, 1958.

Meyer, Jason C. *The End of the Law: Mosaic Covenant in Pauline Theology.* Nashville: B. & H. Academic, 2009.

Moo, Douglas J. *The Epistle to the Romans.* NICNT. Grand Rapids: Eerdmans, 1996.

Morris, Leon. *The Epistle to the Romans.* Grand Rapids: Eerdmans, 2012.

————. *Galatians: Paul's Charter of Christian Freedom.* Downers Grove: InterVarsity, 1996.

Moule, H. C. G. *The Epistle of St. Paul to the Romans.* London: Pickering & Inglis, 1910.

Murray, John. *Principles of Conduct: Aspects of Biblical Ethics.* Grand Rapids: Eerdmans, 2003.

Peterson, David. *Possessed By God: A New Testament Theology of Sanctification and Holiness.* NSBT. Downers Grove: InterVarsity, 2000.

Pink, Arthur W. *The Ten Commandments.* Grand Rapids: Baker, 1994.

Ridderbos, Herman N. *The Epistle of Paul to the Churches of Galatia.* Grand Rapids: Eerdmans, 1984.

Rooker, Mark F. *The Ten Commandments: Ethics for the Twenty-First Century.* NAC Studies in Bible & Theology 7. Nashville: B. & H. Academic, 2010.

Rosner, Brian S. *Paul and the Law: Keeping the Commandments of God.* NSBT. Downers Grove: InterVarsity, 2013.

————. *Paul, Scripture, and Ethics: A Study of 1 Corinthians 5–7.* Leiden, Netherlands: Brill, 1994.

Schreiner, Thomas R. *40 Questions about Christians and Biblical Law.* 40 Questions, edited by Benjamin L. Merkle. Grand Rapids: Kregel, 2010.

————. *The Law and Its Fulfillment: A Pauline Theology of Law.* Grand Rapids: Baker, 1998.

Seifrid, Mark A. *Christ, Our Righteousness: Paul's Theology of Justification.* NSBT. Downers Grove: Apollos, 2000.

Seitz, Christopher. "The Ten Commandments: Positive and Natural Law and the Covenants Old and New—Christian Use of the Decalogue and

Moral Law." In *I Am the Lord Your God: Christian Reflections on the Ten Commandments*, edited by Carl E. Braaten and Christopher R. Seitz, 18–38. Grand Rapids: Eerdmans, 2005.

Simpson, E. K. *The Pastoral Epistles*. London: Tyndale, 1954.

Smiles, Vincent M. *The Gospel and the Law in Galatia: Paul's Response to Jewish-Christian Separatism and the Threat of Galatian Apostasy*. Collegeville, MN: Liturgical, 1998.

Stifler, James M. *The Epistle to the Romans: A Commentary, Logical and Historical*. Chicago: Moody, 1960.

Stott, John R. W. *Guard the Truth: The Message of 1 Timothy and Titus*. Downers Grove: InterVarsity, 1996.

———. *The Message of Acts: To the Ends of the Earth*. The Bible Speaks Today. Leicester: InterVarsity, 2005.

Tannehill, Robert C. *Dying and Rising with Christ: A Study in Pauline Theology*. Berlin: Töpelmann, 1967.

Thielman, Frank. *Paul & the Law: A Contextual Approach*. Downers Grove: InterVarsity, 1994.

Towner, Philip H. *The Letters to Timothy and Titus*. NICNT. Grand Rapids: Eerdmans, 2009.

Turner, Max. *The Holy Spirit and Spiritual Gifts: In the New Testament Church and Today*. Rev. ed. Peabody, MA: Hendrickson, 1998.

VanGemeren, Willem. "The Law is the Perfection of Righteousness in Jesus Christ: A Reformed Perspective." In *Five Views on Law and Gospel*, edited by Stanley N. Gundry, 13–69. Counterpoints. Grand Rapids: Zondervan, 1996.

Vine, W. E. *1 Corinthians*. Grand Rapids: Zondervan, 1961.

Vos, Howard Frederic. *Galatians: A Call to Christian Liberty*. Chicago: Moody, 1971.

Wakefield, Andrew Hollis. *Where to Live: The Hermeneutical Significance of Paul's Citations from Scripture in Galatians 3:1–14*. Leiden, Netherlands: Brill, 2003.

Waltke, Bruce. "The Kingdom of God in the Old Testament: The Covenants." In *The Kingdom of God: Theology in Community*, edited by Christopher W. Morgan and Robert A. Peterson, 73–94. Wheaton, IL: Crossway, 2012.

Weir, David A. *The Origins of the Federal Theology in Sixteenth-Century Reformation Thought*. Oxford: Clarendon, 1990.

Wellum, Stephen. "Baptism and the Relationship Between the Covenants." In *Believer's Baptism: Signs of the New Covenant in Christ*, edited by Thomas R. Schreiner et al., 97–161. Nashville: B. & H. Academic, 2006.

Wesley, John. *Explanatory Notes upon the Old Testament*. Salem, OH: Schmul, 1975.

———. *Three Sermons on the Original, Nature, Properties, and Use of the Law: And Its Establishment Thro' Faith*. London: Whitfield, 1798.

Westerholm, Stephen. *Perspectives Old and New on Paul: The "Lutheran" Paul and His Critics*. Grand Rapids: Eerdmans, 2008.

Westminster Assembly. *The Larger Catechism of the Westminster Assembly: With Proofs from the Scriptures.* Philadelphia: Presbyterian Board of Education, 1800.

Witherington, Ben. *The Acts of the Apostles: A Socio-Rhetorical Commentary.* Grand Rapids: Eerdmans, 2009.

————. *Grace in Galatia: A Commentary on St. Paul's Letter to the Galatians.* Grand Rapids: Eerdmans, 1998.

————. *Letters and Homilies for Hellenized Christians.* Downers Grove: IVP Academic, 2006.

Wuest, Kenneth Samuel. *Romans in the Greek New Testament for the English Reader.* Grand Rapids: Eerdmans, 1955.

Author Index

Scripture Index